Henry W Sayen

The Grand International Centennial Chess Congress

Held in Philadelphia, in August, 1876, during the celebration of the American centennial

Henry W Sayen

The Grand International Centennial Chess Congress
Held in Philadelphia, in August, 1876, during the celebration of the American centennial

ISBN/EAN: 9783337221478

Printed in Europe, USA, Canada, Australia, Japan

Cover: Foto ©Suzi / pixelio.de

More available books at **www.hansebooks.com**

THE

GRAND INTERNATIONAL

CENTENNIAL CHESS CONGRESS,

HELD IN

PHILADELPHIA,

IN

August, 1876,

DURING

THE CELEBRATION OF THE AMERICAN CENTENNIAL.

EDITED BY

W. HENRY SAYEN.

ANNOTATED BY

JACOB ELSON, B. M. NEILL, AND W. H. SAYEN.

I have gathered together a nosegay of choice flowers, and have nothing of my own but the thread which unites them.

PHILADELPHIA:
CLAXTON, REMSEN, AND HAFFELFINGER,
1876.

COLLINS, PRINTER,
705 Jayne Street.

HISTORY OF THE TOURNAMENT.

NEAR the close of the year 1875, at the annual meeting of the PHILADELPHIA CHESS CLUB, held on Dec. 10, the President, Mr. Jos. M. Bennett, in his able address, after stating the various objects for which the Club had been instituted, and more especially for the advancement of the interests of the game of Chess, recommended that in no way could those interests be better subserved than by the holding of a Grand International Tournament in Philadelphia during the Centennial year 1876. Mr. G. Henderson thereupon moved that the Board of Managers of the Club for that year be empowered and have full authority to carry out the various suggestions made in the message of the President; and the motion was carried unanimously.

In accordance therewith, the Board of Managers met on December 20, 1875, and after organizing themselves into a Centennial Committee of the Philadelphia Chess Club, with power to add to their numbers, elected Mr. Jos. M. Bennett, President; Geo. C. Helmbold, Vice-President; W. H. Sayen, Secretary; and Emerson Bennett, Treasurer; and at once decided to issue the following call:—

Whereas, The Philadelphia Chess Club has been frequently importuned, by numerous chess organizations throughout the country, to hold a tournament under its auspices during the centennial year; therefore,

Resolved, That the Philadelphia Chess Club offers playing accommodations and the sum of two hundred and fifty dollars, at least, as a nucleus for a fund for a Grand International Chess Tournament, to be held under the auspices of the Philadelphia Chess Club during the Centennial Exposition of 1876.

Resolved, That in accordance with the above resolution, the Centennial Board of Management of the Philadelphia Chess Club requests each club organization subscribing to this tournament to select one member as a representative of such organization in the said Board, to arrange rules of playing, distributing prizes, etc.

Resolved, That we cordially invite the co-operation and assistance of the chess players and admirers of the game throughout the world.

This call was cordially responded to by the St. Louis Chess Club, represented by Mr. Max Judd, and the Boston Chess Club, represented by Messrs. P. Ware, Jr., and J. B. Rhodes, who at once started subscription lists in the cities named. Mr. Ware also issued a call to the governors of States, which was responded to by Governor Garland, of Arkansas, in the shape of a very handsome Silver Cup. Messrs. Mackenzie, Barnett, and Mason, of New York, and Mr. H. E. Bird, of London, also promised material aid and co-operation; whilst Cleveland under Messrs. J. F. White and J. B. McKim,

Detroit under Mr. T. P. Bull, and Hartford under Mr. J. G. Belden, swung rapidly into line. Some scattering assistance was promised from various other sections of the country, but it amounted to very little, as probably the universal stagnation of business throughout the country produced a like apathy among the chess players of the land.

However, the energy of those interested in the movement never flagged, and though the sums subscribed were not equal to what was expected, yet sufficient was realized to make the Tournoi a complete success.

A committee of three members was now appointed, viz.: Messrs. Jacob Elson, W. H. Sayen, and L. D. Barbour, who were instructed to draft the rules and regulations of play, and, after a careful examination of the laws of all previous tournaments, they decided on issuing the following general rules:—

Rules and Regulations of Play of the Grand Centennial International Chess Tournament. To be held in Philadelphia, August, 1876.

1st. The Tournament will commence on August 15th, 1876.

2d. All entrance fees must be paid to the Treasurer by July 15th, 1876.

3d. The entrance fee shall consist of twenty dollars, and accompanying each entrance fee must be the additional sum of ten dollars, which will be held as a pledge that each contestant will play out all his games; and on his failure to do so, the forfeit will be retained or returned to him, as the committee may decide.

4th. The rules and regulations of play, as published in *Staunton's Chess Praxis*, will be exclusively followed in this Tourney, and all the games must be played in rooms chosen by the committee.

5th. The time limit shall be twelve moves an hour, by the sand glass, for each player.

6th. Each player shall contest two games with every other player, and drawn games will count as half games for each player.

7th. The hours for play shall be from 9 A.M. until 1 P.M., and from 2 until 6 P.M., and from 7.30 P.M. until midnight; and each of these three divisions shall be called a sitting.

8th. Each contestant will be required to play at least three sittings in two days.

9th. If an entire game be finished in less time than one sitting, it will be considered the same as one entire sitting for each player, and it will remain optional with either of them as to whether they play more or not during that sitting.

10th. All disputes must be referred to the committee, and their decisions will be final.

11th. The player winning the greatest number of games will be declared the victor, and entitled to first choice of prizes; the player winning the next greatest, the second, etc.

12th. All ties shall be played off by two games between the parties, or lots may be cast, as the contestants themselves may elect.

JACOB ELSON,
W. H. SAYEN, } *Committee.*
L. D. BARBOUR,

N. B.—The amounts of the various prizes will not be published until July 15th, 1876, when the subscription list will be closed.

To the above were added the following, which were passed at the general meeting of the players, just before the commencement of play, on August 15th, 1876:—

1st. The play shall begin on August 15, at 10 P. M., and at that hour all entrance fees must be paid.

2d. In making up the score, if any player, for any reason, omits to play the number of games allotted to him, then his games shall only be counted for or against those who have played with him, and shall not count for or against those who have not played with him.

3d. The committee on awards and reference shall consist of three members, viz.: Messrs. W. H. Sayen, Emerson Bennett, and W. H. Helmbold.

4th. The decision of any one member of the committee, in the absence of the others, shall be final in all disputes.

5th. The winner shall hand in the full score of each game to one of the committee within twenty-four hours of its being played. If the game be drawn, then the player having first move shall hand in the score, under the following penalties: 1st. If he win the game, it will not be counted for him; 2d. If drawn, it will be counted against him.

6th. The names of the players shall be written separately on slips of paper, and placed in a receptacle, and drawn one by one, and they shall play with each other in the order drawn, two and two.

7th. The money shall be divided into five prizes, and the silver cup shall go with the first prize.

8th. The committee shall announce the amounts of the prizes on Monday, August 21.

9th. The player having the move at the end of the sitting shall write his move before leaving the table, and place it in a sealed envelope, and hand it to one of the committee or their substitutes, and his time in making such move will be counted against him.

10th. A player coming in one hour after the commencement of the sitting will forfeit the game, subject, however, to an appeal to the committee, who, if his excuse be valid, may decide otherwise.

11th. The games shall be the exclusive property of the association for publication in book form, each player, however, being entitled to the use of three of his games for that purpose.

On August 15, the following gentlemen had entered their names for the grand contest:—

L. D. BARBOUR, of Philadelphia, a very brilliant player, whose reputation is well known over the country for great originality.

H. E. BIRD, of London, the strongest living native English player, whose fame dates from the Chess Congress of 1851, which he entered as a very young man, contending successfully against the greatest masters, and, in 1866, losing a match to Steinitz, the champion of Europe, by a score of 7 to 5. Mr. Bird might be called the knight-errant of chess.

HARRY DAVIDSON, of Philadelphia, probably the most brilliant player in the country, the youngest contestant, of indomitable pluck and daring style.

JACOB ELSON, of Philadelphia, a veteran chess player and problemist, a profound and thorough player, a great student, and one whose reputation is well known in this country and in Europe.

MAX JUDD, of St. Louis, the champion of the West, who first contended in the Chicago Tournament in 1873, showing evidence of great chess power, which he subsequently proved by defeating Mr. Alberoni in a match in 1875, after the latter had won his great victory over Mr. Ensor, and when he was considered at the height of his fame.

D. M. MARTINEZ, of Havana, the champion of Cuba, a player finished in style and masterly in combination, who defeated Captain Mackenzie in New York in 1874, by the odd game. Owing to sickness in his family, Mr. Martinez was compelled to withdraw after playing four games, and the chess world lost some specimens of very fine play.

JAS. MASON, of New York, of world-wide reputation, a player who combines both soundness and brilliancy, qualities rarely united. Mr. Mason has won many notable victories, and has long been anxious to cross swords with the masters of Europe.

ALBERT ROBERTS, of Philadelphia, who first gave indications of fine play during the visit of Messrs. Mackenzie and Bird to Philadelphia in February, 1876, when he contested some very fine games. Mr. Roberts may one day rise to great eminence in chess.

P. WARE, Jr., of Boston, the champion of New England, a warm friend, a gallant gentleman, and always ready for the fray. Mr. Ware's pleasant manners did much to enliven the play.

This was undoubtedly the finest collection of chess talent ever brought together in this country, whilst the amounts of the prizes, aggregating as they did over $1000, rendered the Tournoi a magnificent success.

Where all engaged were so active, it would be almost invidious to distinguish, but I cannot help paying a fitting tribute to the vast energy of Messrs. Jos. M. Bennett, the President; Emerson Bennett, the Treasurer; Wm. H. Helmbold, Jacob Elson, Jas. Abbott, of Philadelphia, Max Judd, of St. Louis, and P. Ware, Jr., of Boston, to whose untiring efforts the success of the Tournoi was mainly due.

Play commenced on Wednesday, August 16, at 9 A. M., with the following gentlemen paired: L. D. Barbour *vs.* Max Judd; H. E. Bird *vs.* Jas. Mason; H. Davidson *vs.* D. M. Martinez; Jacob Elson *vs.* P. Ware, Jr.; and was continued for fourteen days, excluding Sundays, until August 31; and so evenly were the contestants matched, that the first prize was uncertain until the last game was played. During the whole of this period not a dispute or unpleasantness of any kind occurred, and only the best of good feeling was manifested. Many distinguished strangers visited the rooms and witnessed the play, notably those two veterans of chess, Messrs. Perrin, of New York, and Maurian, of New Orleans; and the games were, with few exceptions, the finest ever witnessed in this country.

At the close of play on August 31, 1876, the following was

THE OFFICIAL SCORE.

	Barbour.	Bird	Davidson.	Elson.	Judd.	Martinez.	Mason.	Roberts.	Ware.	Games won.
Barbour,	×	0½	00	00	00	×	½0	00	½½	2
Bird,	1½	×	1½	0½	10	×	0½	11	1½	8½
Davidson,	11	0½	×	0½	1½	½½	10	1½	01	9
Elson,	11	1½	1½	×	0½	×	0½	½½	10	8
Judd,	11	01	0½	1½	×	×	0½	11	11	9½
Martinez,	×	×	½½	×	×	×	00	×	×	1
Mason,	½1	1½	01	1½	1½	11	×	1½	11	12½
Roberts,	11	00	0½	½½	00	×	0½	×	½1	5½
Ware,	½½	0½	10	01	00	×	00	½0	×	4
Games lost	12	5½	7	6	4½	3	3½	8½	10	Total 60

SUMMARY.

	Won.	Lost.
Barbour	2	12
Bird	8½	5½
Davidson	9	7*
Elson	8	6
Judd	9½	4½
Martinez	1	3*
Mason	12½	3½*
Roberts	5½	8½
Ware	4	10

In accordance with the above score, the committee on awards, appointed by unanimous consent, consisting of

* Davidson and Mason, having been the only contestants against Martinez, their scores counted—Mason 10½ won, 3½ lost; and Davidson 8 won, 6 lost—which accounts, under the rules, for Elson tying the latter.

Messrs. W. H. Sayen, W. H. Helmbold, and Emerson Bennett, made the following official announcement of the division of the prizes:—

First Prize, Mr. Jas. Mason, of New York, consisting of $300 and Gov. Garland's silver cup.

Second Prize, Mr. Max Judd, of St. Louis, consisting of $200 and a handsome gold medal, appropriately inscribed.

Third Prize, Mr. H. E. Bird, of London, consisting of $150 and a handsome gold medal, appropriately inscribed.

Fourth Prize, Mr. Jacob Elson,* consisting of $100 and a handsome gold medal, appropriately inscribed.

Fifth Prize, Mr. H. Davidson,* consisting of $50 and a handsome gold medal, appropriately inscribed.

Sixth Prize, Mr. Albert Roberts, of Philadelphia, consisting of $8 and a handsome gold medal, appropriately inscribed.

Four of the medals were the gift of Mr. Jos. M. Bennett, and one the gift of Mr. A. Herzberg, of Philadelphia. The players, on receipt of their several prizes, expressed themselves appropriately, and passed, by acclamation, a unanimous vote of thanks to the Committee for their courteous, kind, and impartial treatment of them.

* Mr. Elson and Davidson were tied for fourth and fifth prizes. They played off, each winning one, and the book went to press before it was decided.

The following is a complete list of the subscribers to the Tournament, with the amounts subscribed, together with the total amount of expense incurred from Dec. 20, 1875, to August 31, 1876, taken from the official records of the treasurer:—

FROM PHILADELPHIA.

Jos. M. Bennett	$85 00
Richard L. Willing	50 00
Jas. Abbott	25 00
J. A. Kaiser	25 00
J. L. Ringwalt	10 00
A. Herzberg	10 00
Jno. Walker, Jr.	10 00
David Balsley	10 00
J. Garitee (part ent. fee L. D. Barbour)	10 00
Jas. G. Whiteman	10 00
Jas. S. Martin	10 00
John Dawson	10 00
Wm. C. Walker	5 00
N. Burt	5 00
R. R. Montgomery	5 00
Lewis Elkin	5 00
A. E. Dougherty	5 00
Cash	5 00
"	1 00
"	1 00
Wm. Wolff	1 00
J. W. Jackson	1 00
E. Law	1 00
Jacob Elson (E. F.)	20 00
H. Davidson "	20 00
A. Roberts "	20 00
L. D. Barbour " See J. Garitee	10 00
Total	$370 00

St. Louis.

Max Judd (subscribed and collected from friends)	$165 00
Max Judd (E. F.)	20 00
Total	$185 00

Boston.

P. Ware, Jr. (subscribed and collected from friends)	$33 50
J. Fairweather	50 00
P. Ware, Jr. (E. F.)	20 00
Total	$103 50

Detroit.

T. P. Bull	$5 00
D. C. Rogers	10 00
W. E. Quimby	5 00
W. Blair	2 00
Cash	1 00
Total	$23 00

New York.

Jas. Mason (E. F.)	$20 00
E. H. Underhill (per Capt. Mackenzie)	10 00
Total	$30 00

Cleveland.

J. G. White	$20 00
J. B. McKim	5 00
Total	$25 00

Hartford.

Jno. G. Belden	$10 00
Mrs. J. W. Gilbert	10 00
Total	$20 00

SCATTERING.

Dr. J. P. Barnett, Brooklyn, L. I. .	$25 00
C. C. Barnes, Canajoharie, N. Y. . .	10 00
Henry Bird (E. F.), London, Eng. . .	20 00
D. M. Martinez (E. F.), Havana, Cuba .	20 00
C. A. Maurian, New Orleans, La. . .	10 00
Eugene B. Cook, Hoboken, N. J. . .	5 00
"Miron" and "Phania," Compton Villa, N. H.	5 00
F. M. Peterson, Vera Cruz, Mexico .	5 00
G. S. Peck	5 00
Total	$105 00

SUMMARY.

Philadelphia	$370 00
St. Louis	185 00
Boston	103 50
New York	30 00
Cleveland	25 00
Detroit	23 00
Hartford	20 00
Scattering	105 00
	$861 50
Deduct expenses for circulars, stationery, postage, etc.	53 50
Balance divided into prizes . . .	$808 00

The above is a true exhibit of the financial management of the Tournament, and we venture to state that the expenses were less than ever before in a Tournoi of the same dimensions, covering, as it did, a period of over eight months, from Dec. 20, 1875, to August 31, 1876.

It will also be seen that Boston, St. Louis, and Philadelphia did the main share of the work, Philadelphia alone raising nearly one-half of the grand total subscribed. Chicago and Cincinnati are not represented by a single subscription; whilst New York, which *claims* to be the chess centre of the country, and to which we looked for great assistance, sent but $10 outside of Mr. Mason's entrance fee. Despite, however, all these incomprehensible and annoying discouragements, and their concurrent evils, a lack of support and sympathy from the rest of the chess public, the committee never swerved from their purpose, but carried it through to a successful and gratifying conclusion.

We now close this brief record of the Tournoi with our thanks to those who have assisted us in the work, and with many expressions of regard for the Chess Public, both of this country and of Europe, hoping that the effort here revealed may bear rich fruit in the dissemination of the knowledge of this noblest of games, Chess —and that American Chess may take the high rank in the opinion of European players which this work proves it deserves.

THE EDITOR.

PHILADELPHIA, Oct 2, 1876.

CONTENTS.

PAGE

Barbour *vs.* Bird 113
" " Davidson 95
" " Elson 158
" " Judd 34
" " Mason 73
" " Roberts 50
" " Ware 131

Bird *vs.* Barbour 111
" " Davidson 179
" " Elson 182
" " Judd 139
" " Mason 25
" " Roberts 90
" " Ware 59

Davidson *vs.* Barbour 97
" " Bird 168
" " Elson 108, 198
" " Judd 63
" " Martinez 31
" " Mason 160
" " Roberts 135
" " Ware 187

	PAGE
Elson *vs.* Barbour	155
" " Bird	185
" " Davidson	116
" " Judd	164
" " Mason	146
" " Roberts	71
" " Ware	38
Judd *vs.* Barbour	36
" " Bird	124
" " Davidson	67
" " Elson	166
" " Mason	195
" " Roberts	170
" " Ware	98
Mason *vs.* Barbour	81
" " Bird	53
" " Davidson	152
" " Elson	121
" " Martinez	86
" " Roberts	100
" " Ware	174
Martinez *vs.* Davidson	44
" " Mason	83
Roberts *vs.* Barbour	48
" " Bird	93
" " Davidson	118
" " Elson	79

	PAGE
Roberts *vs.* Judd	171
" " Mason	102
" " Ware	148
Ware *vs.* Barbour	128
" " Bird	56
" " Davidson	191
" " Elson	40
" " Judd	104
" " Mason	177
" " Roberts	142

GRAND INTERNATIONAL

CENTENNIAL CHESS CONGRESS.

GAME No. 1.

Played August 16th and 17th, commencing 9 A. M.

TIME, 12 HOURS.

Hollandish Opening.

White (Mr. Bird).	*Black* (Mr. Mason).
1. P. to K. B. 4th. (*a*)	1. P. to K. B. 4th.
2. Kt. to K. B. 3d.	2. Kt. to K. B. 3d.
3. P. to K. 3d.	3. P. to K. 3d.
4. P. to Q. Kt. 3d.	4. B. to K. 2d.
5. B. to Kt. 2d.	5. Castles.
6. P. to Q. 3d.	6. P. to Q. Kt. 3d.
7. B. to K. 2d.	7. B. to Q. Kt. 2d.
8. Castles.	8. P. to Q. B. 4th. (*b*)
9. Kt. to Q. R. 3d.	9. Kt. to Q. R. 3d.
10. P. to Q. B. 4th.	10. Kt. to Q. B. 2d.
11. Q. to K. sq.	11. K. Kt. to K. sq. (*c*)
12. R. to Q. sq.	12. B. to K. B. 3d.
13. P. to Q. 4th. (*d*)	13. Kt. to Q. 3d.
14. Kt. to K. 5th.	14. B. x Kt.
15. Q. P. x B.	15. Kt. to K. 5th. (*e*)
16. Kt. to Kt. sq.	16. Q. to K. 2d.

White (Mr. Bird).	*Black* (Mr. Mason).
17. Kt. to Q. B. 3d.	17. Q. R. to Q. sq.
18. Kt. x Kt.	18. B. x Kt.
19. Q. to Q. B. 3d. (*f*)	19. P. to K. Kt. 4th. (*g*)
20. B. to B. 3d. (*h*)	20. B. x B.
21. R. x B.	21. P. x P. (*i*)
22. P. x P.	22. K. to R. sq.
23. Q. to Q. 3d.	23. Kt. to K. sq. (*j*)
24. R. to K. R. 3d.	24. R. to K. Kt. sq.
25. Q. to K. B. 3d.	25. R. to Q. Kt. sq.
26. R. to Q. 3d. (*k*)	26. R. to K. Kt. 2d.
27. Q. to Q. sq.	27. Kt. to B. 2d.
28. K. R. to K. Kt. 3d.	28. Q. R. to K. Kt. sq.
29. R. x R.	29. R. x R.
30. B. to Q. B. 3d.	30. Kt. to Q. R. 3d.
31. P. to Q. R. 3d.	31. Kt. to Q. Kt. sq.
32. B. to K. sq.	32. Kt. to Q. B. 3d.
33. R. to K. R. 3d.	33. R. to K. Kt. 5th.
34. R. to K. B. 3d.	34. Kt. to Q. 5th.
35. R. to K. B. 2d.	35. Q. to K. R. 5.
36. R. to K. B. sq.	36. Q. to Q. sq. (*l*)
37. P. to K. R. 3d.	37. R. to K. Kt. 3d.
38. B. to Q. B. 3d.	38. Kt. to Q. B. 3d.
39. R. to K. B. 2d.	39. Q. to K. 2d.
40. R. to K. B. 3d.	40. P. to Q. R. 4th.
41. R. to Q. 3d.	41. R. to K. Kt. 2d.
42. B. to K. sq.	42. K. to K. Kt. sq.
43. B. to K. B. 2d.	43. P. to K. R. 3d.
44. Q. to R. 5th.	44. K. to R. 2d.
45. K. to R. 2d.	45. Q. to B. 2d.
46. Q. to Q. sq.	46. Q. to K. 2d.
47. Q. to K. B. 3d.	47. K. to Kt. sq.
48. R. to Q. 6.	48. K. to R. 2d.

White (Mr. Bird).	*Black* (Mr. Mason).
49. Q. to Q. 3d.	49. K. to Kt. sq.
50. Q. to Q. sq. (*m*)	50. K. to R. 2d.
51. Q. to K. sq.	51. Q. to K. sq.
52. R. to Q. 3d.	52. Q. to Q. R. sq.
53. R. to K. Kt. 3d. (*n*)	53. R. x R.
54. K. x R.	54. Kt. to Q. 5th.
55. B. x Kt.	55. P. x B.
56. Q. to Q. 2d. (*o*)	56. Q. to K. 5th.
57. K. to K. B. 2d.	57. K. to K. Kt. 3d.
58. P. to K. Kt. 3d.	58. P. to K. R. 4th.
59. Q. to K. 2d.	59. P. to K. R. 5th.
60. Q. to Q. 2d.	60. P. x P., check.
61. K. x P.	61. Q. to Q. Kt. 8th.
62. Q. x Q. P.	62. Q. x Kt. P., check.
63. K. to K. R. 4th.	63. Q. to Q. Kt. 8th.
64. Q. to K. B. 2d. (*p*)	64. Q. to Q. 6th.
65. Q. x Q. Kt. P.	65. Q. x Q. R. P.
66. Q. to Q. 8th.	66. K. to K. B. 2d. (*q*)
67. Q. to B. 6th, check.	67. K. to K. sq.
68. Q. to R. 8th, check.	68. Q. to K. B. sq.
69. Q. to R. 5th, check.	69. K. to Q. sq.
70. Q. to K. B. 3d.	70. Q. to Q. Kt. 5th.
71. Q. to R. 8th, check.	71. K. to K. 2d.
72. K. to Kt. 5th.	72. Q. to Q. B. 6th.
73. Q. to K. Kt. 2d.	73. P. to Q. R. 5th.
74. K. to Kt. 6th.	74. Q. x P.
75. Q. to K. Kt. 5th, ch.	75. K. to K. sq.
76. Q. to K. R. 4th.	76. Q. to Q. Kt. 5th.
77. Q. to K. B. 2d.	77. P. to Q. R. 6th.
78. P. to K. R. 4th.	78. Q. to Q. Kt. 7th.
79. Q. to Q. B. 5th.	79. P. to Q. R. 7th. (*r*)
80. Q. to Q. B. 8th, check.	80. K. to K. 2.

White (Mr. Bird).	*Black* (Mr. Mason).
81. Q. to Q. B. 5th, check.	81. K. to Q. sq.
82. Q. to K. B. 8th, check.	82. K. to B. 2d.
83. Q. to Q. 6th, check.	83. K. to Kt. 2d.
84. Q. x P., check.	84. K. to Kt. 3d.
85. Q. to Q. 6th, check. (*s*)	85. K. to R. 4th.
86. Q. to B. 5th, check.	86. K. to R. 5th.
87. Q. to B. 4th, check.	87. K. to R. 6th.
88. Q. to B. 5th, check.	88. K. to Kt. 6th.
89. Q. to Kt. 5th, check.	89. K. to B. 6th.
90. Q. to B. 5th, check.	90. K. to Q. 6th.
91. Q. to Q. 6th, check.	91. K. to K. 6th.
92. Q. to B. 5th, check.	92. K. to K. B. 6th (*t*)
93. P. to R. 5th.	93. P. Queens.
94. P. to R. 6th.	94. Q. to Q. 5th. (*u*)
95. Q. x Q.	95. Q. x Q.
96. P. to R. 7th.	96. Q. to Q. sq.
97. K. to Kt. 7th.	97. K. x P.
98. P. Queens.	98. Q. x Q.

And Mr. Bird resigns. (*v*)

NOTES BY W. H. SAYEN.

(*a*) This opening, sometimes called irregular, but known as the "Hollandish," was frequently adopted by Mr. Morphy. Mr. Steinitz has also frequently played it, especially in giving the odds of the Knight.

(*b*) In close openings, where Pawn play seems to be alone satisfactory, a move like this, though apparently weakening the Q. P., does not, in reality, on account of the impossibility of bringing forces to bear upon the weak point.

(*c*) A good move, preparatory to relieving himself of the threatening Bishop at Q. Kt. 2d, which may become troublesome.

(*d*) This move certainly gives Black the command of the Q. R. diagonal with Bishop, besides weakening the K. P. 13th B. x B., and if Kt. retakes 14th Kt. to Kt. 5th, followed by 15th B. to K. B. 3d would have given satisfactory results. It would also have given an opening for the Q. on the King's side.

(*e*) We now prefer Black's game, though the weakness of the Q. P. is here felt.

(*f*) To prevent the threatened P. to Q. 4th. It is evident that if Black now play P. to Q. 4th he will lose a piece.

(*g*) A bold move, and perfectly safe in the present position of the adversary's Queen.

(*h*) To prevent P. to Kt. 5th, which would have proved very embarrassing.

(*i*) P. to Kt. 5th could not now be played on account of 22d R. to Kt. 3d, followed by 23d P. to K. 4th.

(*j*) To prevent Q. to Q. 6th, a dangerous move.

(*k*) We here think the following line of play would have been good:—

26. Q. to R. 5th.	26. R. to Kt. 5th, or anything.
27. K. R. to Q. 3d.	27. R. to K. Kt. 2d.
28. Q. to R. 3d.	28. R. to Q. B., the best.
29. Q. to K. B. 3d.	29. Q. to Q.
30. R. to Q. 6th.	30. R. to Q. B. 2d.
31. R. x K. P., and wins.	

(*l*) All this is very fine, and a grand struggle for position. The last five moves have improved Black's game considerably.

(*m*) Black here proposed a draw, but White declined.

(*n*) This move virtually loses the game. P. to K. Kt. 3d was the correct play.

(*o*) He could not prevent the posting of Black's Queen at K. 5th. The game from this point is a study of great interest.

(*p*) To avoid Q. to K. 5th winning, or K. 8th mate.

(*q*) Neatly played. If Q. x P. White loses the game.

(*r*) Now commences a strenuous attempt at perpetual check, which Mr. Mason eludes by a most beautiful line of play.

(*s*) If he had taken the K. P., he could have given but few more checks, commencing at Q. 5th, as his own K. would be exposed to a counter check.

(*t*) Black has now arrived in safe quarters, in the enemy's country.

(*u*) The winning move.

(*v*) This game may justly be considered one of the gems of the Tournament, and on its result depended in a great measure the *morale* of each of these players in their other games.

GAME No. 2.

Played on August 16th, commencing at 9 A. M

TIME, 5 HOURS 20 MINUTES.

French Defence.

White (Mr. Davidson).	*Black* (Mr. Martinez).
1. P. to K. 4th.	1. P. to K. 3d.
2. P. to Q. 4th.	2. P. to Q. 4th.
3. P. x P.	3. P. x P.
4. K. Kt. to B. 3d.	4. K. Kt. to B. 3d.
5. B. to K. 3d. (*a*)	5. B. to Q. 3d.
6. B. to Q. 3d.	6. Castles.
7. Q. Kt. to Q. 2d.	7. P. to Q. B. 3d.
8. P. to K. R. 3d.	8. Q. to B. 2d.
9. P. to Q. B. 3d.	9. B. to B. 5th.
10. Castles.	10. B. to K. 3d.
11. R. to K. sq. (*b*)	11. Q. Kt. to Q. 2d.
12. Kt. to K. 5th.	12. B. x Kt. (*c*)
13. P. x B.	13. Q. x P. (*d*)
14. B. to Q. B. 5th.	14. Q. to B. 2d.
15. B. x R.	15. R. x B.
16. Kt. to B. 3d.	16. R. to K. sq.
17. B. to B. 2d.	17. P. to K. R. 3d.
18. Q. to Q. 4th.	18. P. to B. 4th.
19. Q. to K. R. 4th.	19. R. to Q. sq.
20. Q. R. to Q. sq.	20. Q. to Kt. 3d.
21. P. to Q. Kt. 4th. (*e*)	21. P. x P.

White (Mr. Davidson).	*Black* (Mr. Martinez).
22. P. x P.	22. Kt. to Kt. sq.
23. Q. to Q. 4th.	23. Q. to R. 3d.
24. B. to Q. 3d.	24. Q. to R. 5th.
25. P. to Kt. 5th.	25. Q. to R. 6th.
26. R. to K. 3d.	26. Q. to R. 4th.
27. Kt. to K. 5th.	27. Kt. to Q. 2d.
28. Kt. x Kt.	28. B. x Kt.
29. P. to Q. R. 4th.	29. P. to R. 3d.
30. R. to Q. B. sq.	30. P. x P.
31. P. x P.	31. R. to Q. R. sq.
32. K. to R. 2d. (*f*)	32. B. x P.
33. B. x B.	33. Q. x B.
34. R. to Kt. 3d.	34. Q. to R. 3d.
35. R. to Q. Kt. sq.	35. Kt. to R. 4th.
36. R. to Q. Kt. 6th.	36. Q. to B. 5th.
37. Q. x Q.	37. P. x Q.
38. R. to K. Kt. 4th.	38. R. to Q. B. sq.
39. R. x K. R. P.	39. P. to K. Kt. 3d. (*g*)
40. R. x Kt.	40. P. to Q. B. 6th.
41. R. from R. 5th to R. 4th.	41. P. to Q. Kt. 4th.
42. R. to K. 4th.	42. P. to B. 7th.
43. R. to K. sq.	43. P. to B. 8th, Queens.
44. R. x Q.	44. R. x R.
45. R. to Q. Kt. 4th.	45. R. to Q. B. 4th.
46. K. to Kt. 3d.	46. P. to B. 3d.
47. K. to B. 3d.	47. R. to K. 4th.
48. R. to K. 4th.	48. R. to Q. B. 4th.
49. K. to K. 3d.	49. K. to B. 2d.
50. K. to Q. 3d.	50. P. to B. 4th.
51. R. to Q. Kt. 4th.	51. K. to K. 3d.
52. P. to K. Kt. 4th.	52. P. x P.
53. P. x P.	53. K. to B. 3d.

White (Mr. Davidson).	*Black* (Mr. Martinez).
54. R. to K. 4th.	54. R. to B. 3d.
55. K. to Q. 4th.	55. P. to Kt. 5th.
56. K. to Q. 3d.	56. R. to B. 6th, check.
57. K. to Q. 2d.	57. R. to K. B. 6th.
58. R. x P.	58. R. x P., check.
59. K. to K. 3d.	59. R. to Q. B. 7th.
60. K. to B. 3d.	60. R. to B. 4th.

61. R. to Q. 4th, and the game was abandoned as drawn.

NOTES BY W. H. SAYEN.

(*a*) B. to Q. 3d is generally played here.

(*b*) 11th Q. R. to B. sq. followed by B. to Kt. sq. and Q. to B. 2d, gives a fine attack, and preserves the K. B. from being exchanged, while threatening, at a future period, B. to R. 2d.

(*c*) B. x B. would have been better.

(*d*) If—	13. Kt. x P.
14. B. to B. 4th.	14. K. Kt. to Q. 2d.
15. B. x Kt.	15. Kt. x B.
16. Q. to R. 5th, and wins.	

Black preferred giving up the exchange to allowing the Pawn to remain at K. 5th.

(*e*) This gives Black a passed pawn, but it being unsupported, may not become dangerous.

(*f*) 32d R. to K. 7th seems to us to have been the proper move here.

(*g*) Well played. The Q. B. P. now becomes worth a Rook.

GAME No. 3.

Played on August 16th, 1876, commencing at 9 A. M.

TIME, 1 HOUR 45 MINUTES.

Irregular Opening.

White (Mr. Barbour).	*Black* (Mr. Judd).
1. P. to K. 3d. (*a*)	1. P. to Q. B. 4th.
2. P. to Q. Kt. 3d.	2. P. to K. 3d.
3. B. to Q. Kt. 2d.	3. Q. Kt. to B. 3d.
4. K. Kt. to B. 3d.	4. K. Kt. to B. 3d.
5. B. to K. 2d. (*b*)	5. P. to Q. 4th.
6. P. to K. R. 3d. (*c*)	6. B. to K. 2d. (*d*)
7. P. to Q. 4th.	7. Castles.
8. Q. Kt. to Q. 2d.	8. B. to Q. 2d.
9. P. to Q. B. 3d.	9. R. to Q. B. sq.
10. Q. to B. 2d.	10. R. to K. sq.
11. Kt. to K. 5th. (*e*)	11. P. x P.
12. K. P. x P.	12. Kt. x Q. P.
13. Q. to Q. 3d.	13. Kt. x B.
14. Q. x B.	14. B. to Q. 3d.
15. Kt. x B.	15. Kt. x Kt.
16. Castles K. R.	16. P. to K. 4th.
17. R. to Q. sq.	17. B. to Kt. sq.
18. P. to K. B. 3d.	18. Q. to B. 2d.
19. K. R. to K.	19. P. to K. 5th.
20. Kt. to B. sq.	20. Kt. to B. 3d.
21. P. to Q. B. 4th.	21. K. P. x P.

White (Mr. Barbour).	*Black* (Mr Judd).
22. Q. x P.	22. R. x R.
23. R. x R.	23. Q. to Kt. 3d, check.
24. K. to R.	24. P. to Q. 5th.
25. Q. to Q. 3d.	25. R. to Q.
26. Kt. to Q. 2.	26. B. to B. 5th.
27. Kt. to B. sq.	27. Q. to R. 4th.
28. R. to R. sq.	28. Q. to K. R. 4th.
29. R. to K. sq.	29. Q. to R. 5th.
30. Q. to Q. sq.	30. Kt. to R. 4th.
31. Q. x P. (*f*)	31. P. to K. R. 3d. (*g*)
32. Q. to K. 4th.	32. Q. to B. 7th.
33. B. to B. sq.	33. B. x B.
34. R. x B.	34. Q. x Kt., check, and wins.

NOTES BY B. M. NEILL.

(*a*) Mr. Barbour's play being of the bold and dashing style, we are surprised at his adopting this move.

(*b*) In close openings this B. is stronger at Q. 3d. White should have played 5th P. to Q. 4th in order to so plant it.

(*c*) We prefer 6th P. to Q. 4th.

(*d*) See note (*b*).

(*e*) An oversight.

(*f*) Natural enough.

(*g*) This quiet move decides the contest in Black's favor.

GAME No. 4.

Played on August 16th, 1876, commencing at 2 P. M.

TIME, 2 HOURS 45 MINUTES.

Irregular Opening.

White (Mr. Judd).	*Black* (Mr. Barbour).
1. P. to Q. B. 4th.	1. P. to K. Kt. 3d. (*a*)
2. P. to K. 3d.	2. B. to Kt. 2d.
3. Q. Kt. to B. 3d.	3. P. to Q. B. 4th.
4. Kt. to B. 3d.	4. Q. Kt. to B. 3d.
5. P. to Q. 4th.	5. P. to Kt. 3d. (*b*)
6. P. to Q. 5th.	6. Kt. to K. 4th.
7. Kt. x Kt.	7. B. x Kt.
8. P. to B. 4th.	8. B. x Kt., check.
9. P. x B.	9. B. to Kt. 2d.
10. P. to K. 4th.	10. P. to K. 4th. (*c*)
11. B. to K. 2d.	11. P. to Q. 3d.
12. Castles.	12. Q. to K. 2d.
13. P. x P.	13. Q. x P.
14. B. to K. B. 4th.	14. Q. to K. 2d.
15. B. to K. Kt. 4th.	15. B. to B.
16. B. x B.	16. R. x B.
17. P. to K. 5th.	17. Q. to Q. 2d. (*d*)
18. P. x P.	18. P. to K. B. 3d.
19. Q. to Q. 2d.	19. K. to B. 2d.
20. Q. R. to K.	20. K. to Kt. 2d.
21. B. to R. 6th, check. (*e*)	21. K. to B. 2d.

White (MR. JUDD).	*Black* (MR. BARBOUR).
22. B. to Kt. 5th.	22. R. to K.
23. R. x R.	23. Q. x R.
24. R. to K.	24. Q. to Q. 2d.
25. Q. to B. 4th.	25. Q. to B. 4th.
26. Q. x Q.	26. P. x Q.
27. B. to B. 4th.	27. K. to B.
28. P. to Q. 7th, and wins.	

NOTES BY B. M. NEILL.

(*a*) P. to Q. Kt. 3d, P. to K. 3d, or P. to Q. B. 4th, are considered stronger.

(*b*) Bad. P. to K. 3d was the move.

(*c*) Black's game is so inferior that no good move seems possible. This game does not improve matters.

(*d*) P. x P., followed eventually by P. to B. 3d, and K. to B. 2d, was Black's only hope.

(*e*) Well played. Mr. Judd conducts the entire game admirably.

GAME No. 5.

Played on August 16th, 1876, commencing at 9 A.M.

TIME, 2 HOURS 45 MINUTES.

Centre Counter Gambit.

White (Mr. Elson).	*Black* (Mr. Ware).
1. P. to K. 4th.	1. P. to Q. 4th.
2. P. x P.	2. Q. x P.
3. Kt. to Q. B. 3d.	3. Q. to Q. sq.
4. B. to B. 4th.	4. P. to Q. B. 3d.
5. Kt. to K. B. 3d.	5. B. to Kt. 5th. (*a*)
6. B. x P., check.	6. K. to Q. 2d. (*b*)
7. Kt. to K. 5th, check.	7. K. to B.
8. Q. x B., check.	8. K. to B. 2d.
9. B. x Kt.	9. R. x B.
10. Q. to K. 6th.	10. Q. to Q. 3d.
11. Q. x Q. (*c*)	11. P. x Q.
12. Kt. to B. 3d.	12. Kt. to Q. 2d.
13. Castles.	13. B. to K. 2d.
14. P. to Q. 4th.	14. P. to K. R. 3d.
15. B. to B. 4th.	15. Kt. to B. 3d.
16. K. R. to K. sq.	16. K. to Q. 2d.
17. Q. R. to Q. sq.	17. P. to K. Kt. 4th.
18. B. to Kt. 3d.	18. P. to Q. R. 3d.
19. Kt. to K. 4th.	19. Kt. to R. 4th.
20. P. to Q. B. 4th.	20. Q. R. to K. B.
21. P. to Q. B. 5th.	21. Kt. x B.

White (Mr. Elson).	*Black* (Mr. Ware).
22. B. P. x Kt.	22. P. to Kt. 5th.
23. P. x P.	23. B. x P.
24. Kt. to K. 5th, check.	24. K. to B. 2d.
25. Kt. x B.	25. K. x Kt.
26. R. to K. B.	26. R. x R., check.
27. R. x R.	27. K. to Q. 4th.
28. R. to B. 4th.	28. P. to Q. B. 4th.
29. R. x P.	29. R. to Q. B.
30. Kt. to B. 3d.	30. R. to B. 3d.
31. P. x P.	31. R. x P.
32. R. to Q. 4th, check.	32. K. to K. 3d.
33. R. to K. 4th, check.	33. K. to B. 3d.
34. R. to Q. Kt. 4th.	34. P. to Q. Kt. 4th.
35. P. to Q. R. 4th.	35. P. x P.
36. R. x P.	36. R. to B. 8th, check.
37. K. to B. 2d.	37. R. to B. 7th, check.
38. K. to B. sq.	38. R. x P.
39. R. x P., check, and wins.	

NOTES BY JACOB ELSON.

(*a*) Inconsiderate. B. to K. B. 4th seems to be the correct move at this point, and was adopted by Mr. Ware in his games at this opening with the other players of the tournament.

(*b*) It would of course have been better to take the B. The move adopted loses a clear piece. In any case, however, White had a winning game.

(*c*) The safest move, and better than taking R. The remainder now is only a question of time.

GAME No. 6.

Played on August 17th, 1876, commencing at 9 A.M.

TIME, 5 HOURS.

Irregular Opening.

White (Mr. P. Ware).	*Black* (Mr. J. Elson).
1. P. to Q. 4th.	1. P. to K. B. 4th.
2. P. to K. B. 4th.	2. P. to K. 3d.
3. Kt. to K. B. 3d.	3. Kt. to K. B. 3d.
4. P. to K. 3d.	4. P. to Q. Kt. 3d.
5. B. to K. 2d.	5. B. to Kt. 2d.
6. Castles.	6. B. to K. 2d.
7. Kt. to K. 5th.	7. Castles.
8. B. to B. 3d.	8. Kt. to K. 5th.
9. P. to Q. B. 4th.	9. P. to Q. 3d.
10. Kt. to Q. 3d.	10. Kt. to Q. 2d.
11. Kt. to Q. B. 3d.	11. Q. to Kt. B. 3d.
12. Kt. to B. 2d.	12. P. to Q. 4th.
13. Q. Kt. x Kt.	13. Kt. x Kt.
14. B. x Kt.	14. B. P. x B.
15. P. to Q. Kt. 3d.	15. B. to R. 3d.
16. Q. to B. 2d.	16. R. to Q. B. sq.
17. R. to K. sq.	17. P. to Q. B. 4th.
18. B. to Kt. 2.	18. B. P. x P.
19. B. x P.	19. B. to B. 3d.
20. Q. to R. Q.	20. B. to Kt. 2d.
21. Q. to K. 2d.	21. Q. to K. 2d.

White (Mr. P. Ware).	*Black* (Mr. J. Elson).
22. P. x P.	22. P. x P.
23. Kt. to Kt. 4th.	23. B. x B.
24. R. x B.	24. R. to B. 2d.
25. P. to K. Kt. 3d.	25. K. R. to Q. B. sq.
26. K. R. to Q. sq.	26. R. to B. 7th.
27. Q. R. to Q. 2d.	27. Q. to Q. B. 4th.
28. Kt. to K. 5th.	28. R. x R.
29. Q. x R.	29. Q. to B. 6th. (*a*)
30. K. to B. 2d.	30. Q. x Q., check. (*b*)
31. R. x Q.	31. K. to B.
32. P. to K. Kt. 4th.	32. K. to K. 2d.
33. P. to Kt. 5th.	33. K. to K. 3d.
34. K. to Kt. 3d.	34. R. to B. 6th.
35. K. to B. 2d.	35. R. to B. 2d. (*c*)
36. P. to K. R. 3d.	36. B. to B.
37. P. to K. R. 4th.	37. B. to Kt. 2d.
38. R. to Kt. 2d.	38. K. to B. 4th.
39. R. to Q. 2.	39. B. to R. sq.
40. P. to R. 5th.	40. B. to Kt. 2d.
41. K. to Kt. 3d.	41. R. to B. 6th.
42. K. to B. 2d.	42. R. to B. 2d.
43. K. to K. 2d.	43. B. to R. sq.
44. K. to B.	44. R. to B. 6th.
45. K. to K. 2d.	45. R. to B. 2d.
46. P. to Kt. 6th.	46. P. x P.
47. P. x P.	47. B. to Kt. 2d.
48. R. to Kt. 2d.	48. B. to R. sq.
49. R. to Q. 2d.	49. B. to Kt. 2d.
50. P. to Q. Kt. 4th.	50. P. to Kt. 4th.
51. Kt. to B. 7th (*d*)	51. B. to R. sq.
52. Kt. to Q. 6th, check.	52. K. x P.
53. Kt. x P.	53. R. to B. 5th.

4*

White (Mr. P. Ware).	*Black* (Mr. J. Elson).
54. P. to R. 3d.	54. P. to R. 3d.
55. Kt. to Q. 4th.	55. R. to B. 2d.
56. R. to B. 2d.	56. R. x R. (*e*)
57. Kt. x R.	57. B. to B. 3d.
58. K. to Q. 2d.	58. K. to B. 3d.
59. K. to B. 3d.	59. P. to Kt. 4th.
60. P. x P.	60. K. x P.
61. Kt. to Q. 4th.	61. B. to Q. 2d.
62. Kt. to K. 2d.	62. K. to Kt. 5th. (*f*)
63. K. to Q. 4th.	63. K. to B. 6th.
64. Kt. B. 3d.	64. B. to B. 3d.
65. P. to Q. R. 4th.	65. B. to Q. 2d.
66. P. to Kt. 5th.	66. P. x P.
67. P x P.	67. B. to K. sq.
68. P. to Kt. 6th.	68. B. to B. 3d.
69. Kt. to Kt. 5th, and wins.	

NOTES BY JACOB ELSON.

(*a*) In the hope of inducing White to take Q. at once, which would have given Black a marked advantage.

(*b*) Q. to Q. R. 8th, a threatening-looking move, was inadmissible, as White in reply would have made the fine move of R. x Q. P.

(*c*) Black, having the fear of theory "before his eyes," which declares that a Kt. in similar positions is preferable to a B., is anxious to draw. A more enterprising line of play in the next dozen moves might have led to a different result. At the present moment, B. to Q. R. 3d, threatening R. to B. 8th, would have been a good strong move, and should have been adopted.

(*d*) Well played. Intending on K. x P. to play Kt. to Q. 6th, threatening to capture the B. and afterwards the Q. P. with the R. and also attacking Q. Kt. P. Black can indeed defend both points by B. to B. 3d, but White would, in that case, reply with R. to B. 2d, cramping Black's game fearfully.

(*e*) A serious error of judgment; Black should not have exchanged Rooks.

(*f*) A more disastrous error than the last. The only hope of a draw was in bringing the K. back to B. 3d, and then over to the Q. side.

GAME No. 7.

Played on August 17th, 1876, commencing at 9 A. M.

TIME, 4 HOURS.

Hollandish Opening.

White (Mr. Martinez).	*Black* (Mr. Davidson).
1. P. to Q. 4th.	1. P. to K. B. 4th.
2. P. to K. 4th (*a*)	2. P. x P.
3. Kt. to Q. B. 3d.	3. Kt. to K. B. 3d.
4. B. to K. Kt. 5th.	4. P. to Q. 3d.
5. B. x Kt.	5. K. P. x B.
6. Kt. x K. P.	6. P. to K. B. 4th.
7. Kt. to Q. B. 3d.	7. B. to K. 3d.
8. Q. to K. 2d.	8. K. to B. 2d.
9. Castles.	9. B. to K. 2d.
10. R. to K. sq.	10. B. to Kt. 4th, check.
11. K. to Kt. sq.	11. R. to K. sq.
12. P. to Q. 5th.	12. B. to Q. 2d.
13. Q. to R. 5th check.	13. K. to Kt. sq. (*b*)
14. R. x R. check.	14. B. x R.
15. Q. to K. B. 3d.	15. B. to K. Kt. 3d.
16. B. to Q. 3d.	16. Q. to B. 3d. (*c*)
17. P. to K. Kt. 3d.	17. Kt. to Q. 2d.
18. Q. to Q. sq.	18. Q. to B. 2d.
19. P. to K. B. 4th.	19. B. to B. 3d.
20. K. Kt. to K. 2d.	20. Kt. to Kt. 3d.
21. R. to K. B. sq.	21. R. to K. sq.

White (Mr. Martinez).	*Black* (Mr. Davidson).
22. P. to Q. R. 4th.	22. B. to K. R. 4th.
23. P. to Q. R. 5th. (*d*)	23. Q. B. x Kt.
24. B. x B.	24. B. x Kt. (*e*)
25. P. x Kt.	25. B. to Q. 5th.
26. B. to Q. Kt. 5th.	26. R. to K. 5th.
27. Q. to Q. 2d.	27. B. x P.
28. R. to K. sq.	28. Q. to K. 2d.
29. R. to K. 2d.	29. R. x R.
30. B. x R.	30. Q. to K. 6th. (*f*)
31. Q. x Q.	31. B. x Q.
32. P. to Q. B. 4th.	32. B. to K. Kt. 8th.
33. P. to K. R. 3d.	33. B. to R. 7th.
34. P. to K. Kt. 4th.	34. P. x P.
35. B. x P.	35. B. x B. P.
36. K. to B. 2.	36. K. to B. 2d.
37. P. to Q. Kt. 4th.	37. K. to B. 3d.
38. B. to B. 8th.	38. P. to Q. Kt. 3d.
39. P. to Q. Kt. 5th. (*g*)	39. K. to K. 4th.
40. K. to Q. 3d.	40. P. to K. R. 4th.
41. B. to K. 6th.	41. P. to K. Kt. 4th.
42. B. to B. 7th.	42. P. to K. Kt. 5th.
43. P. x P.	43. P. to R. 5th.
44. B. to Kt. 6th.	44. P. to R. 6th.
45. B. to K. 4th.	45. P. to R. 7th.
46. B. to R. sq.	46. B. to Kt. 4th.
47. B. to B. 3d.	47. K. to B. 5th.
48. K. to K. 2d.	48. K. to Kt. 6th.
49. B. to K. 4th.	49. K. x P.
50. B. to R. sq.	50. K. to B. 5th.
51. B. to Kt. 2d.	51. K. to K. 4th.
52. K. to Q. 3d.	52. K. to B. 3d.
53. K. to K. 4th.	53. K. to K. 2d.

White (Mr. Martinez).	*Black* (Mr. Davidson).
54. K. to K. 4th.	54. B. to B. 3d.
55. B. to B. 3d.	55. B. to K. 4th.
56. B. to R. sq.	56. K. to Q. 2d.
57. K. to Q. 3d.	57. K. to B. sq.
58. K. to B. 2d.	58. K. to Kt. 2d.
59. K. to Kt. 3d.	59. P. to Q. R. 4th.
60. P. x P. (en pass), ch.	60. K. x P.
61. K. to R. 4th.	61. K. to Kt. 2d.
62. K. to Kt. 4th.	62. K. to B. sq.
63. K. to Kt. 3d.	63. K. to Q. 2d.
64. K. to B. 2d.	64. K. to K. 2d.
65. K. to Q. 3d.	65. K. to B. 3d.
66. K. to K. 2d.	66. K. to B. 4th.
67. B. to Kt. 2d.	67. K. to B. 5th.
68. B. to R. sq.	68. B. to Q. 5th.
69. B. to Kt. 2d.	69. B. to B. 3d.
70. B. to R. sq.	70. B. to Q. sq.
71. B. to Kt. 2d.	71. K. to K. 4th.
72. K. to Q. 3d.	

And the game was abandoned as drawn.

NOTES BY W. H. SAYEN.

(*a*) This is the first time we have seen this move played. If Black attempts to retain the pawn, it yields a fine attack to White, yet we cannot consider the sacrifice sound, though Mr. Martinez, being ill, did not make the most of it. *Vide* first game between Messrs. Mason and Martinez.

(*b*) Mr. Davidson played well in getting into safe quarters so soon.

(*c*) At this point we prefer Black's game, on account of the threatening position of the two Bishops, and the possibilities involved in the attack with the Queen's Pawns.

(*d*) This advance of the Q. R. P. might be considered very injudicious by some, but it seemed to be the only method of saving the threatened Q. P.

(*e*) Well played.

(*f*) This exchange was ill-considered, as the Bishops are of opposite colors, and Black, though a pawn ahead, cannot hope for more than a draw.

(*g*) It now seems to be impossible to do aught but draw. Black should have played P. to Q. R. 4th, before bringing forward his King.

GAME No. 8.

Played on August 17th, 1876, commencing at 9 A. M.

TIME, 1 HOUR.

Petroff's Defence.

White (Mr. Roberts).	*Black* (Mr. Barbour).
1. P. to K. 4th.	1. P. to K. 4th.
2. Kt. to K. B. 3d.	2. Kt. to K. B. 3d.
3. Kt. x P.	3. P. to Q. 3d.
4. Kt. to K. B. 3d.	4. Kt. x P.
5. P. to Q. 4th.	5. P. to Q. 4th.
6. B. to Q. 3d.	6. B. to Q. 3d. (*a*)
7. Castles.	7. Castles.
8. P. to Q. B. 4th.	8. P. to Q. B. 3d.
9. Q. to B. 2d.	9. P. to K. B. 4th.
10. P. x P.	10. P. x P.
11. Q. to Kt. 3d.	11. K. to R. sq.
12. Kt. to B. 3d.	12. Kt. to Q. B. 3d.
13. K. to R. sq. (*b*)	13. Kt. x Kt.
14. P. x Kt.	14. B. to K. 2d.
15. B. to K. B. 4th.	15. P. to Q. R. 3d.
16. Q. R. to K. sq.	16. P. to Q. Kt. 4th.
17. Kt. to K. 5.	17. Kt. to R. 4th.
18. Q. to Kt. sq.	18. P. to K. Kt. 4th.
19. B. to Q. 2d.	19. P. to K. B. 5th. (*c*)
20. B. x R. P.	20. R. to B. 3d.
21. B. to Q. 3d.	21. Kt. to B. 5th.

White (Mr. Roberts).	*Black* (Mr. Barbour).
22. B. x Kt.	22. Kt. P. x B.
23. Kt. to Kt. 6th, check.	23. R. x Kt.
24. Q. x R.	24. Q. to B. sq.
25. R. to K. 5th.	25. B. to B. 3d. (*d*)
26. R. to K. 8th.	

And after a few more moves, Black resigned.

NOTES BY W. H. SAYEN.

(*a*) Weak. Correct play is Kt. to K. B. 3d, followed by B. to K. 2d.

(*b*) Best. Threatening to win the Q. P.

(*c*) Objectless. No attack can be expected from these Pawns.

(*d*) Mr. Barbour was laboring under severe indisposition when playing this game.

GAME No. 9.

Played on August 17th, 1876, commencing at 11 A. M.

TIME, 2 HOURS 20 MINUTES.

Ruy Lopez's Knight's Game.

White (Mr. Barbour).	*Black* (Mr. Roberts).
1. P. to K. 4th.	1. P. to K. 4th.
2. Kt. to K. B. 3d.	2. Kt. to Q. B. 3d.
3. B. to Q. Kt. 5th.	3. P. to Q. R. 3d.
4. B. to R. 4th.	4. Kt. to K. B. 3d.
5. Castles.	5. P. to Q. Kt. 4th. (*a*)
6. B. to Kt. 3d.	6. Kt. x K. P.
7. B. to Q. 5th. (*b*)	7. Kt. to K. B. 3d.
8. B. x Q. Kt.	8. Q. P. x B.
9. Kt. x K. P.	9. B. to Kt. 2d.
10. R. to K. sq.	10. B. to K. 2d.
11. P. to Q. Kt. 4th. (*c*)	11. Castles.
12. B. to Kt. 2d.	12. B. x Kt. P.
13. Kt. to Kt. 4th.	13. B. to K. 2d.
14. R. x B. (*d*)	14. Q. x R.
15. Kt. x Kt.	15. P. x Kt.
16. P. to Q. 3d.	16. P. to K. B. 4th.
17. Kt. to Q. 2d.	17. P. to Q. B. 4th.
18. Q. to R. 5th.	18. Q. to K. 3d.
19. Kt. to B. sq.	19. Q. to Kt. 3d.
20. Kt. to Kt. 3d.	20. Q. R. to K. sq. (*e*)
21. P. to K. B. 4th (*f*)	21. R. to K. 6th.
22. Q. to R. 3d.	22. K. R. to K. sq.

White (Mr. Barbour).	*Black* (Mr. Roberts).
23. B. to K. 5th.	23. P. to K. B. 3d.
24. B. x Q. B. P.	24. Q. to Kt. 5th.
25. Q. to R. 5th.	25. R. to K. 8th, check.
26. R. x R.	26. R. x R., check.
27. K. to B. 2d.	27. R. to K. 7th, check.
28. K. to B. sq.	28. B. x P., check.
29. K. to Kt. sq.	29. Q. x Q.
30. Kt. x Q.	30. K. to B. 2d.
31. P. to Q. B. 3d.	31. B. to R. 6th.
32. P. to R. 3d.	32. R. to Kt. 7th, check.
33. K. to R. sq.	33. K. to Kt. 3d.
34. Kt. to Kt. 3d.	34. P. to K. R. 4th.
35. B. to Q. Kt. 6th.	35. P. to R. 5th.
36. Kt. to B. sq.	36. R. to B. 7th.
37. Kt. to K. 3d.	37. R. to K. 7th.
38. Kt. to B. sq.	38. R. to K. 8th.
39. B. x P.	39. R. x Kt., check.
40. B. to Kt. sq.	

And Black announced mate in four moves. (*g*)

NOTES BY W. H. SAYEN.

(*a*) We prefer to this move the regular one of 5. Kt. x K. P.

(*b*) We think a stronger game can be obtained by 7. P. to Q. 4th, *i. e.*:—

7. P. to Q. 4th.	7. B. to K. 2d, best.
8. R. to K. sq.	8. P. to Q. 4th.
9. Kt. x K. P.	9. Kt. x Kt.
10. P. x Kt.	10. B. to Kt. 2d.
11. Kt. to Q. 2d.	11. Kt. x Kt.
12. B. x Kt.	12. Castles.
13. P. to K. B. 4th.	13. B. to B. 4th, check.
14. K. to R. sq.	14. B. to Kt. 3d.

15. P. to Q. B. 3d, and we prefer White's game.

(*c*) These posthumous Evans Gambits generally lead to loss for those who attempt them. P. to Kt. 3d would have been equally effective.

(*d*) He should first have played P. to K. R. 3d, when, if the Bishop were not removed, the combination would have been sound, as Q. to Kt. 4th, check, followed by Q. to B. 5th would win after taking the Kt.

(*e*) He evidently could not take the Queen without serious loss.

(*f*) 21. P. to K. B. 3d would have been much better, as he would then have threatened 22. Q. x K. B., P.

(*g*) As follows:—

	40. K. to R. 4th.
41. P. to Q. 4th.	41. K. to Kt. 5th.
42. P. to Q. 5th.	42. K. to B. 6th.
43. P. to Q. 6th.	44. B. to Kt. 7th, mate.

GAME No. 10.

Played on August 17th, 1876, commencing at 9 A. M.

TIME, 3 HOURS 30 MINUTES.

King's Bishop Gambit.

White (Mr. Mason).	*Black* (Mr. Bird).
1. P. to K. 4th.	1. P. to K. 4th.
2. P. to K. B. 4th.	2. P. x P.
3. B. to B. 4th.	3. Kt. to K. B. 3d. (*a*)
4. Kt. to Q. B. 3d.	4. B. to Q. Kt. 5th.
5. P. to K. 5th.	5. P. to Q. 4th.
6. B. to Kt. 3d. (*b*)	6. Kt. to K. 5th.
7. Kt. to B. 3d.	7. B. to K. 3d.
8. Q. to K. 2d.	8. B. x Kt.
9. Kt. P. x B.	9. Kt. to Q. B. 3d.
10. Castles.	10. Castles. (*c*)
11. P. to Q. B. 4th.	11. Kt. to Kt. 4th.
12. Kt. x Kt.	12. Q. x Kt.
13. P. x P.	13. Kt. to Q. 5th.
14. Q. to B. 2d.	14. Kt. x B.
15. R. P. x Kt.	15. B. x P.
16. P. to Q. 4th.	16. Q. to Kt. 3d.
17. B. x B. P.	17. P. to Q. Kt. 4th. (*d*)
18. K. R. to K. sq.	18. P. to Q. B. 3d.
19. R. to K. 3d.	19. K. R. to K. sq.
20. Q. R. to K. sq. (*e*)	20. P. to K. B. 3d,
21. R. to K. Kt. 3d. (*f*)	21. Q. to B. 2d.

White (Mr. Mason).	*Black* (Mr. Bird).
22. P. x P.	22. Q. x P.
23. B. to K. 5th.	23. Q. x Q., check.
24. K. x Q.	24. R. to K. 2d.
25. K. to K. 3d.	25. P. to Q. B. 4th.
26. K. to Q. 2d.	26. Q. R. to K. sq.
27. Q. R. to K. 3d.	27. P. to K. Kt. 3d.
28. B. to Q. 6th.	28. R. x R.
29. R. x R.	29. R. x R.
30. K. x R.	30. P. x P., check.
31. K. x P.	31. B. x K. Kt. P.
32. K. to B. 5th.	32. K. to B. 2d. (*g*)
33. B. to Kt. 8th.	33. P. to Kt. 4th.
34. B. x P.	34. K. to Kt. 3d.
35. K. to Q. 4th. (*h*)	35. K. to B. 4th.
36. K. to K. 3d.	36. K. to Kt. 5th.
37. K. to B. 2d.	37. B. to B. 3d.
38. B. to Kt. 8th.	

And the game was abandoned as drawn.

NOTES BY W. H. SAYEN.

(*a*) First played by Ruy Lopey in 1561, not recommended as highly as 3. P. to Q. 4th.

(*b*) The Handbuck here gives 6. B. to Kt. 5th, check, and follows :—

	6. P. to Q. B. 3d.
7. P. x Kt.	7. P. x B.
8. Q. to K. 2d, check.	8. B. to K. 3d.

9. Q. x Kt. P., check, and gives White the best game.

(*c*) We think Kt. to B. 4th first would have been stronger, as the exchanging of the dangerous K. B. is always good in this gambit.

(*d*) A good move at this juncture. We can do no better than to recommend the reader to study carefully the preceding six moves.

(*e*) We should here have preferred P. to Q. Kt. 4th, followed by 21. K. R. to Q. R. 3d, and commenced an assault on the weak Q. R. P., but the Bishops being of opposite colors, even though the Pawn should fall, in the event of an exchange of pieces taking place during its capture, the game would, from its nature, be drawn.

(*f*) If P. x P. then follows—

	21. R. x R.
22. R. x R.	22. Q. x. P.
23. B. to K. 5th.	23. Q. to Kt. 3d.

And Black has a slight advantage.

(*g*) He could not save the Pawn, *i. e.*—

	32. B. to B. 8th.
33. B. to Q. Kt. 8th.	33. P. to Q. R. 4th.
34. B. to B. 7th.	34. P. to R. 5th.
35. P. x P.	35. P. x P.

36. K. to Kt. 4th, and White remains with a passed Pawn.

(*h*) Taking the Pawn would have been of no avail, the Bishop being of opposite colors.

GAME No. 11.

Played on August 18th, 1876, commencing at 9 A. M.

TIME, 3 HOURS 30 MINUTES.

Irregular Opening.

White (MR. WARE).	*Black* (MR. BIRD).
1. P. to Q. 4th.	1. P. to K. B. 4th.
2. P. to K. B. 4th.	2. Kt. to K. B. 3d.
3. Kt. to K. B. 3d.	3. P. to K. 3d.
4. P. to K. 3d.	4. P. to Q. Kt. 3d.
5. B. to K. 2d.	5. B. to Kt. 2d.
6. P. to Q. R. 3d.	6. B. to K. 2d.
7. P. to Q. B. 3d.	7. Castles.
8. Castles.	8. Q. to K. sq.
9. Kt. to K. 5th.	9. P. to Q. 3d.
10. B. to B. 3d.	10. P. to Q. B. 3d.
11. Kt. to Q. 3d.	11. Kt. to K. 5th.
12. Kt. to Q. 2d.	12. P. to Q. 4th (*a*)
13. B. to K. 2d. (*b*)	13. Kt. to Q. 2d.
14. Kt. to K. B. 3d.	14. B. to Q. 3d.
15. Kt. from Q. 3d to K. 5th.	15. Q. Kt. to K. B. 3d.
16. B. to Q. 2d.	16. K. to R. sq.
17. B. to K. sq.	17. B. x Kt.
18. Kt. x B.	18. Kt. to Q. 2d.
19. Kt. to B. 3d.	19. P. to Q. R. 4th.
20. Q. R. to Q. B. sq.	20. P. to Q. R. 5th.
21. Kt. to Q. 2d.	21. Kt. x Kt.

White (Mr. Ware).	*Black* (Mr. Bird).
22. Q. x Kt.	22. P. to Q. Kt. 4th.
23. B. to B. 3d.	23. Kt. to Kt. 3d.
24. Q. to K. 2d. (*c*)	24. B. to R. 3d.
25. Q. to K. B. 2d. (*d*)	25. Kt. to B. 5th.
26. R. to Q. B. 2d.	26. Q. to K. 2d.
27. B. to K. 2d.	27. Kt. to Q. 3d.
28. B. to Q. 3d.	28. R. to B. 3d (*e*)
29. Q. to B. 3d.	29. R. to R. 3d.
30. P. to K. Kt. 4th. (?)	30. P. x P.
31. Q. x P.	31. P. to Kt. 5th.
32. Q. to Q. sq.	32. B. x B.
33. Q. x B.	33. P. x Q. R. P.
34. P. x P.	34. R. to Kt. 3d, check.
35. K. to R. sq.	35. Kt. to B. 5th.
36. P. to K. 4th.	36. Q. x R. P.
37. P. to K. 5th.	37. Q. to K. 2d.
38. R. to R. 2d.	38. P. to R. 6th.
39. P. to B. 5th.	39. P. x P.
40. Q. x P.	40. Kt. to K. 6th.
41. Q. to B. 7th.	41. Q. x Q.
42. R. x Q.	42. Kt. to B. 5th.
43. B. to Kt. 3d.	43. P. to K. R. 4th.
44. R. to B. 5th.	44. R. to Q. Kt. sq.
45. R. x P., check.	45. K. to Kt. sq.
46. R. to B. 5th.	46. R. to Kt. 7th.
47. R. to B. 2d.	47. R. to K. Kt. 5th.
48. K. to Kt. 2d. (*f*)	48. R. to K. 5th
49. K. to R. 3d. (*g*)	49. R. to K. 6th.
50. R. to Kt. 2d.	50. R. x Q. R.
51. R. x R.	51. R. x Q. B. P.
52. K. to Kt. 4th.	52. K. to B. 2d.
53. K. to B. 5th.	53. R. to B. 6th, check.

White (Mr. Ware).	*Black* (Mr. Bird).
54. K. to Kt. 4th.	54. R. to Q. 6th.
55. K. to B. 5th.	55. P. to Kt. 3d, check.
56. K. to Kt. 5th.	56. R. to Q. 7th.
57. R. to R. sq.	57. P. to R. 7th.
58. R. to K. B. sq., check.	58. K. to K. sq.
59. P. to K. 6th.	59. R. to Kt. 7th.
60. R. to Q. R. sq.	60. Kt. to Q. 7th.
61. K. x P.	61. Kt. to Kt. 6th.
62. R. to K. B. sq.	62. P. Queens, and wins.

NOTES BY W. H. SAYEN.

(*a*) The opening moves do not show much advantage for either side. We slightly prefer Black's game.

(*b*) Weak play, as Kt. to K. 5 is equally good now, as the Q. Kt. can go to B. 3d afterwards. We would prefer P. to Q. Kt. 4th, followed by B. to Kt. 2d, after first exchanging the K. B. for the Kt. at K. 5th, and then playing Kt. to K. 5th. *i. e.*—

13. B. x Kt.	13. B. P. x B.
14. Kt. to K. 5th.	14. Kt. to Q. 2d.
15. P. to Q. Kt. 4th, etc.	

(*c*) He should never have allowed the Kt. to play to Q. B. 5th.

(*d*) White's last two moves are very weak.

(*e*) 28. P. to Q. Kt. 5th might here have been played, for if B. x B. then

	29. P. to Kt. 6th.
30. R. to B. sq.	30. R. x B.

and plants the Kt. at K. 5th with a fine game.

(*f*) P. to K. 6th, followed by 49. B. to K. 5th, should Rook play to K. 5th would perhaps have been better.

(*g*) Threatening R. x Q. R. P.

GAME No. 12.

Played on August 18th, 1876, commencing at 2 P. M.

TIME, 7 HOURS.

Centre Counter Gambit.

White (Mr. Bird).	*Black* (Mr. Ware).
1. P. to K. 4th.	1. P. to Q. 4th.
2. P. x P.	2. Q. x P.
3. Kt. to Q. B. 3d.	3. Q. to Q. sq.
4. P. to Q. 4th.	4. P. to Q. B. 3d.
5. B. to K. 3d.	5. B. to B. 4th.
6. B. to Q. 3d.	6. B. x B.
7. Q. x B.	7. P. to K. 3d. (*a*)
8. K. Kt. to K. 2d.	8. Kt. to K. B. 3d.
9. Castles, K. R.	9. B. to Q. 3d.
10. P. to K. R. 3d.	10. Q. Kt. to Q. 2d.
11. B. to Kt. 5th.	11. B. to K. 2d.
12. Kt. to Kt. 3d.	12. Q. to B. 2d.
13. Q. Kt. to K. 2d.	13. P. to K. R. 3d.
14. B. to B. 4th.	14. B. to Q. 3d.
15. B. x B.	15. Q. x B.
16. Q. to Kt. 3d.	16. Castles, K. R.
17. Q. R. to Q. sq. (*b*)	17. Q. to Q. B. 2d.
18. P. to Q. B. 4th.	18. Q. R. to Q. sq.
19. P. to B. 5th.	19. P. to Q. Kt. 3d.
20. P. x P.	20. P. x P.
21. R. to Q. B. sq.	21. Kt. to Q. 4th. (*c*)

White (Mr. Bird).	*Black* (Mr. Ware).
22. K. R. to K. sq.	22. Q. Kt. to B. 3d.
23. R. to Q. B. 2d.	23. Q. to Q. 3d.
24. K. R. to Q. B. sq.	24. Q. R. to Q. B. sq.
25. P. to Q. R. 3d.	25. R. to B. 2d.
26. Kt. to B. 3d.	26. K. R. to Q. B. sq.
27. Kt. x Kt.	27. Kt. x Kt.
28. Kt. to K. 4th.	28. Q. to B. 5th.
29. Q. to Q. 3d.	29. Q. to B. 4th.
30. Q. to K. 2d. (*d*)	30. Kt. to B. 5th.
31. Q. to K. 3d.	31. Kt. to Q. 4th.
32. Q. to K. sq.	32. Kt. to B. 5th.
33. Kt. to Kt. 3d.	33. Q. to Q. 4th.
34. Q. to K. 4th.	34. Q. to Q. 3d.
35. Kt. to K. 2d.	35. Kt. to Q. 4th. (*e*)
36. P. to K. Kt. 3d.	36. P. to Q. Kt. 4th.
37. Kt. to B. 3d.	37. P. to Kt. 5th. (*f*)
38. P. x P.	38. Kt. x P.
39. R. to Q. 2d.	39. K. R. to Q. sq.
40. R. to K. sq.	40. Q. to Q. 2d.
41. Q. to Kt. 4th.	41. K. to R. sq.
42. K. R. to Q. sq.	42. Q. to K. 2d.
43. Q. to K. 2d.	43. R. to Q. R. sq.
44. Kt. to K. 4th.	44. Kt. to Q. 4th.
45. Kt. to B. 5th.	45. R. to Q. R. 4th.
46. R. to Q. B. sq.	46. R. to Kt. 4th.
47. R. to Q. R. sq.	47. R. to Q. R. 2d.
48. R. fr. Q. 2d to Q.	48. Q. to B. 2d.
49. R. x R.	49. Q. x R.
50. Kt. to K. 4th.	50. Q. to Kt. sq.
51. R. to Q. 2d.	51. R. to Kt. 6th.
52. K. to Kt. 2d.	52. K. to Kt. sq.
53. Kt. to B. 5th.	53. R. to Kt. 4th.

White (Mr. Bird).	*Black* (Mr. Ware).
54. R. to B. 2d.	54. Kt. to Kt. 5th.
55. R. to Q. 2d.	55. Q. to Q. 3d.
56. K. to R. 2d.	56. Q. to Q. 4th.
57. Kt. to K. 4th.	57. Q. to Q. sq.
58. Kt. to B. 3d.	58. R. to Kt. 3d.
59. Q. to B. 4th.	59. Q. to Q. 2d.
60. P. to K. R. 4th.	60. Kt. to Q. 4th.
61. Q. to K. 2d.	61. R. to Kt. 6th.
62. Kt. to K. 4th.	62. R. to Kt. 5th.
63. Kt. to B. 5th.	63. Q. to K. 2d.
64. Q. to Q. R. 6th.	64. Q. to Q. B. 2d.
65. Q. to R. 3d.	65. Q. to Q. sq.
66. P. to K. B. 4th.	66. R. to Kt. 4ht.
67. Q. to K. B. 3d.	67. Kt. to K. 2d.
68. Q. to K. 2d.	68. Q. to Q. 4th.
69. P. to Kt. 4th.	69. Q. to Q. 3d.
70. Q. to K. 5th.	70. Q. to Q. 4th.
71. Q. to K. 3d.	71. R. to R. 4th.
72. R. to Q. B. 2d.	72. P. to K. R. 4th.
73. P. to B. 5th.	73. Q. to Q. 3d, check.
74. Q. to K. 5th.	74. Q. x Q., check.
75. P. x Q.	75. K. P. x P.
76. Kt. P. x R. P.	76. K. to R. 2d.
77. P. to Q. Kt. 4th.	77. R. to Kt. 4th.
78. R. to B. 4th.	78. K. to R. 3d.
79. P. to K. 6th.	79. P. x P.
80. Kt. x P.	80. R. to K. 4th.
81. Kt. to Q. 4th.	81. R. to Q. 4th.
82. Kt. x P.	82. Kt. x Kt.
83. R. x Kt., check.	83. K. x R. P.
84. R. to B. 4th.	84. P. to Kt. 3d.

White (Mr. Bird).	*Black* (Mr. Ware).
85. K. to Kt. 3d.	85. R. to Q. 6th, check.
86. K. to Kt. 2d.	86. P. to Kt. 4th.
87. P. x P.	87. K. x P.

And the game was drawn.

NOTES BY W. H. SAYEN.

(*a*) All the advantages in the opening are with White, who has a much better developed game.

(*b*) It is evident that he gains nothing by taking the Q. Kt. P.

(*c*) Black has played the latter moves with admirable precision, and secured a very good position.

(*d*) It is evident if he takes the Pawn with Rook he loses a piece at least.

(*e*) The game is played with such caution that there is nothing on which to comment.

(*f*) Well played.

GAME No. 13.

Played on August 18th, 1876, commencing at 9 A.M.

TIME, 4 HOURS.

Sicilian Defence.

White (Mr. Davidson).	*Black* (Mr. Judd.)
1. P. to K. 4th.	1. P. to Q. B. 4th.
2. Kt. to K. B. 3d.	2. P. to K. 3d.
3. Kt. to Q. B. 3d.	3. Kt. to Q. B. 3d.
4. P. to Q. 4th.	4. P. x P.
5. Kt. x P.	5. K. Kt. to K. 2d. (*a*)
6. B. to K. 2d. (*b*)	6. P. to Q. 4th.
7. Castles. (*c*)	7. Kt. x Kt.
8. Q. x Kt.	8. Kt. to B. 3d.
9. Q. to R. 4th.	9. P. to Q. 5th (*d*)
10. Kt. to Kt. 5th.	10. P. to K. B. 3d. (*e*)
11. P. to Q. B. 3d. (*f*)	11. P. x P.
12. B. to K. B. 4th.	12. P. to K. 4th.
13. Q. R. to Q. sq.	13. B. to Q. 2d. (*g*)
14. B. to K. Kt. 4th.	14. Kt. to Q. 5th.
15. B. x B., check.	15. Q. x B.
16. R. x Kt. (*h*)	16. P. x R.
17. K. to B. 7th, check.	17. K. to Q. sq.
18. Q. x Q., check.	18. K. x Q.
19. Kt. x R.	19. B. to Q. 3d.
20. B. x B.	20. K. x B.
21. P. x P.	21. P. x P.
22. R. to Q. sq., check. (*i*)	22. K. to B. 3d.

White (Mr. Davidson).	*Black* (Mr. Judd).
23. R. to Q. B. sq.	23. R. x Kt.
24. R. x P., check.	24. K. to Kt. 3d.
25. K. to B. sq.	25. R. to Q. sq.
26. K. to K. 2d.	26. R. to Q. 2d.
27. K. to K. 3d.	27. R. to Q. B. 2d.
28. R. to Q. 3d.	28. K. to B. 4th (*j*)
29. P. to B. 4th.	29. P. to Q. Kt. 4th.
30. R. to B. 3d., check.	30. K. to Q. 3d.
31. R. x R.	31. K. x R.
32. K. to Q. 4th.	32. K. to B. 3d.
33. P. to K. 5th. (*k*)	33. P. x P., check.
34. P. x P.	34. P. to Q. R. 3d.
35. P. to K. 6th.	35. K. to Q. 3d.
36. P. to K. 7th.	36. K. x P.
37. K. to B. 5th.	37. K. to K. 3d.
38. K. to Kt. 6th.	38. K. to Q. 4th.
39. K. x R. P.	39. K. to B. 4th. (*l*)
40. K. to Kt. 7th.	40. P. to Kt. 5th.
41. K. to B. 7th.	41. K. to Kt. 4th.
42. K. to Q. 6th.	42. K. to R. 5th.
43. K. to B. 6th.	43. K. to R. 4th.
44. K. to B. 5th.	44. K. to R. 5th.
45. K. to Kt. 6th.	45. P. to Kt. 6th.
46. P. x P., check.	46. K. x P.
47. K. to B. 5th.	47. K. to B. 6th.
48. K. to Q. 6th.	48. K. to Q. 5th.
49. K. to K. 6th.	49. K. to K. 6th.
50. K. to B. 7th.	50. K. to B. 7th.
51. K. x P.	51. K. x P.
52. P. to R. 4th.	52. P. to R. 4th.
53. K. to Kt. 6th.	53. K. to Kt. 6th.
54. K. x P.	54. K. to B. 5th.

55. K. to Kt. 6th, and Mr. Judd resigned. (*m*)

NOTES BY W. H. SAYEN.

(*a*) Weak in the extreme. The correct move there is Kt. to K. B. 3d, as the attack of K. Kt. to Kt. 5th is now considered weak, as the following variation (an American discovery) will show:—

	5. Kt. to K. B. 3d.
6. K. Kt. to Kt. 5th.	6. B. to Q. Kt. 5th.
7. Kt. to Q. 6th, check.	7. K. to K. 2d.
8. B. to K. B. 4th.	8. P. to K. 4th.
9. Kt. to B. 5th, check.	9. K. to B.
10. B. to Kt. 5th.	10. Q. to R. 4th.

And Black now threatens to play 11. P. to Q. 4th with terrible effect; but again Mr. Steinitz recommends for White 6. P. to K. Kt. 3d, followed by 7. B. to K. Kt. 2d, and thinks that White obtains a fine game, so that the Sicilian Defence has yet to be proved effective against the best play.

(*b*) P. to K. Kt. 3d would, we think, have been stronger play, as it would have rendered dangerous the advance of Black Q. P.

(*c*) Decidedly good. Black dare not take the K. P. on account of the threatened reply of 8. K. Kt. to Q. Kt. 5th.

(*d*) Compulsory. If he take the Pawn, R. to Q. followed by Kt. to Kt. 5th, would be indefensible, and if he suffer the Pawn to be isolated, it must eventually be lost.

(*e*) To avoid the fatal effects of B. to K. B. 4th.

(*f*) Well played! Black has no choice, but to take the Pawn.

(*g*) The only move. It is very evident the Queen cannot be moved.

(*h*) A blunder. He should here have played—

16. Kt. to B. 7th, check.	16. K. to Q.
17. Q. x Q., check.	17. K. x Q.
18. Kt. x R.	18. B. to Q. 3d, best.
19. B. to K. 3d.	19. Kt. to K. 7th, check.
20. K. to R.	20. K. to K. 2d, best.
21. P. x P.	

And White must win as Black dare not take the B. P. with Kt. on account of R. to Q. B. sq., which would eventually release the Kt. at Q. R. 8th.

(*i*) Winning the Pawn by force, as Black must play K. to B. 3d to keep the Knight from escaping.

(*j*) We do not think it was good policy on the part of Black to thus court the exchange of Rooks.

(*k*) A brilliant conception.

(*l*) A fatal error. K. to B. 3d would have retained the opposition, which would have drawn the game.

(*m*) Mr. Davidson's play, from the 39th move was a fine specimen of end play, and without error.

GAME No. 14.

Played August 18th, 1876, commencing at 4.30 P.M.

TIME, 5 HOURS.

Irregular Opening.

White (Mr. Judd).	*Black* (Mr. Davidson).
1. P. to Q. B. 4th.	1. P. to K. B. 4th. (*a*)
2. P. to K. 3d.	2. Kt. to K. B. 3d.
3. Kt. to Q. B. 3d.	3. P. to Q. 3d.
4. P. to Q. 4th.	4. P. to K. 3d.
5. K. Kt. to B. 3d.	5. B. to K. 2d.
6. B. to Q. 3d.	6. Q. Kt. to B. 3d.
7. Castles.	7. Castles.
8. Kt. to Q. 2d. (*b*)	8. P. to K. 4th.
9. P. to Q. 5th.	9. Q. Kt. to Kt. 5th.
10. B. to K. 2d.	10. Kt. to R. 3d.
11. P. to K. B. 3d. (*c*)	11. Q. to K. sq.
12. P. to K. 4th. (*d*)	12. P. to B. 5th.
13. Kt. to Kt. 3d.	13. Q. to Kt. 3d.
14. K. to B. 2d. (*e*)	14. Kt. to R. 4th.
15. K. to K. (*f*)	15. Q. x P.
16. K. to Q. 2d.	16. B. to R. 6th. (*g*)
17. Q. to K. sq.	17. P. to K. Kt. 3d.
18. R. to R. sq. (*h*)	18. Q. R. to Kt. sq. (*i*)
19. P. to Q. R. 3d.	19. B. to Q. 2d.
20. K. to B. 2d.	20. P. to Q. Kt. 4th.
21. P. x P.	21. R. x P.

White (Mr. Judd).	*Black* (Mr. Davidson).
22. Kt. x R.	22. B. x Kt.
23. K. to Q. sq.	23. B. x B., check.
24. Q. x B.	24. Q. x R., check.
25. K. to B. 2d.	25. Q. to Kt. 8th. (*j*)
26. Q. x Kt.	26. Q. to B. 7th, check. (*k*)
27. Kt. to Q. 2d.	27. Kt. to B. 3d.
28. P. to Kt. 4th.	28. P. to K. R. 4th.
29. B. to Kt. 2d.	29. P. to K. Kt. 4th.
30. P. to K. R. 3d.	30. P. to Kt. 5th.
31. R. to K. B. sq.	31. Q. to K. 6th.
32. R. P. x P.	32. P. x P.
33. P. x P.	33. Kt. x K. P.
34. Kt. x Kt.	34. Q. x Kt., check.
35. Q. to Q. 3d.	35. Q. to Kt. 7th, check. (*l*)
36. K. to Kt. 3d.	36. P. to K. 5th.
37. Q. to B. 4th.	37. R. to B. 2d.
38. B. to Q. 4th.	38. B. to Kt. 4th. (*m*)
39. Q. to B. 6th.	39. B. to R. 3d.
40. R. to K. Kt. sq.	40. Q. to R. 6th, check.
41. K. to R. 4th.	41. P. to B. 6th.
42. P. to Kt. 5th.	42. B. to B.
43. P. to Kt. 6th.	43. R. to K. 2d.
44. P. to Kt. 7th.	44. B. x P.
45. B. x B.	45. R. x B.
46. Q. to K. 8th, check.	46. K. to R. 2d.
47. Q. x K. P., check.	47. K. to R.
48. Q. to K. 8th, check.	48. K. to R. 2d.

And the game was abandoned as drawn.

NOTES BY W. H. SAYEN.

(*a*) Mr. Steinitz considers this move weak in most openings, yet Mr. Morphy frequently played it with success. We think its weakness has yet to be demonstrated.

(*b*) Withdrawing this Kt. to the Queen's side, as was afterwards done, was not commendable, as it weakened the defences of the King.

(*c*) Weak. 11. P. to Q. Kt. 3d, followed by 12. B. to Kt. 2d, would have been better play. The move in the text hampers the K. B., and cripples his game.

(*d*) Again very unwise play. B. to Q. 3d was much better.

(*e*) K. to R. would have been answered by 14. Kt. to R. 4th, 15. Kt. to Kt. 6th, check, but we think the move in the text was better than R. to B. 2d, as Black would have at once advanced the K. R. P., and it is difficult to see how White could escape loss.

(*f*) Compulsory. R. to Kt. sq. would have been answered by

	15. B. to R. 5th, check.
16. K. to B. sq.	16. Kt. to Kt. 6th, check.
17. P. x Kt.	17. Q. x P., and wins.

(*g*) We here prefer 16. B. to R. 5th, followed by 17. B. to B. 7th, with a fine game.

(*h*) If 18. R. to Kt., the following might ensue:—

	18. Q. x K. R. P.
19. R. to R. sq.	19. Q. to Kt. 7th.
20. R. to Kt. sq.	20. B. to K. R. 5th.
21. Q. x B.	21. Q. x R.
22. Q. x B.	22. Kt. to Kt. 6th.
23. Kt. to Q. sq.	23. Kt. to Q. Kt. 5th.
24. P. to Q. R. 3d.	24. Kt. x B.
25. P. x Q. Kt.	25. Kt. to Q. 5th.
26. Kt. x Kt.	26. Q. x Kt., check.

And wins two Pawns, leaving a force of 8 Pawns to four and the exchange.

(*i*) The commencement of a fine combination.

(*j*) The only move to save the Queen.

(*k*) He should have played Q. x R. P., check, followed by Q. to

B. 7th. An attempt to force a game like the present one, is almost always futile.

(*l*) Again the opportunity for winning is thrown away; he should have played—

	35. Q. x. Q., check.
36. K. x Q.	36. K. to B. 2d.
37. K. to K. 4th.	37. K. to Kt. 3d.
38. R. to K. R. sq.	38. R. to Q. Kt. sq.
39. R. to R. 2d.	39. K. to Kt. 4th.
40. K. to B. 3d.	40. R. to Kt. 4th.
41. R. to Q. 2d.	41. P. to Q. R. 4th.
42. P. x P.	42. R. x R. P.
43. R. to Q. B. 2d.	43. B. to B. 3d.
44. B. to B. sq.	44. R. to R. 5th.
45. R. x B. P., best.	45. P.,to K. 5th, check.
46. K. to B. 2d.	46. K. x P., and wins.

(*m*) P. to K. 6th was certainly preferable to the move in the text, *i. e.*—

	38. P. to K. 6th.
39. R. x B. P.	39. R. x R.
40. Q. x R.	40. Q. x Q. P., check.
41. K. to B. 3d.	41. P. to K. 7th, and wins.

GAME No. 15.

Played on August 18th, 1876, commencing at 9 A. M.

TIME, 6 HOURS 30 MINUTES.

Ruy Lopez's Knight's Game.

White (Mr. Elson).	*Black* (Mr. Roberts).
1. P. to K. 4th.	1. P. to K. 4th.
2. Kt. to K. B. 3d.	2. Kt. to Q. B. 3d.
3. B. to Kt. 5th.	3. P. to Q. R. 3d.
4. B. to R. 4th.	4. Kt. to K. B. 3d.
5. Kt. to Q. B. 3d.	5. B. to Q. B. 4th.
6. Castles.	6. Castles.
7. P. to Q. 3d.	7. P. to Q. 3d.
8. B. to K. Kt. 5th.	8. Kt. to K. 2d.
9. B. x Kt.	9. P. x B.
10. Kt. to R. 4th.	10. P. to K. B. 4th.
11. Kt. x P.	11. Kt. x Kt.
12. P. x Kt.	12. B. x P.
13. K. to R.	13. B. to Kt. 3d.
14. P. to K. B. 4th.	14. P. to K. B. 4th. (*a*)
15. B. to Kt. 3d, check.	15. K. to R.
16. Q. to K. B. 3d.	16. P. to Q. B. 3d.
17. Q. R. to K. sq.	17. B. to Q. 5th. (*b*)
18. P. x P.	18. B. x P.
19. P. to K. Kt. 3d.	19. Q. to K. Kt. 4th.
20. Q. to K. 3d.	20. Q. to K. R. 4th.
21. P. to Q. 4th.	21. B. to Kt. 2d.

White (Mr. Elson).	*Black* (Mr. Roberts).
22. Kt. to K. 2d. (*c*)	22. Q. R. to K. sq.
23. Q. to Q. 2d.	23. B. to R. 3d.
24. Kt. to K. B. 4th.	24. Q. to Kt. 5th.
25. P. to Q. B. 3d.	25. P. to Q. 4th.
26. B. to Q.	26. Q. to K. Kt. 4th.
27. R. x R.	27. R. x R.
28. R. to K.	28. R. x R., check.
29. Q. x R.	29. Q. to K. B. 3d.
30. B. to B. 3d.	30. Q. to Q. 3d.
31. Kt. x B., check.	31. P. x Kt.
32. Q. to K. 2d.	32. K. to Kt. 2d.
33. K. to Kt. 2d.	33. K. to B. 3d.
34. K. to B. 2d.	34. Q. to K. 2d.
35. Q. x Q., check.	35. K. x Q.
36. K. to K. 2d.	36. B. to B. 8th.
37. P. to Q. Kt. 3d.	37. B. to Kt. 7th.
38. K. to Q. 3d.	

Drawn.

NOTES BY JACOB ELSON.

(*a*) This move seems to give Black the better game.

(*b*) An unexpected and excellent move, requiring great care on the part of White.

(*c*) It was absolutely necessary to bring the Queen's pieces over to the K. side.

GAME No. 16.

Played on August 18th, 1876, commencing at 9 A.M.

TIME, 4 HOURS 30 MINUTES.

Ruy Lopez's Knight's Game.

White (Mr. Barbour).	*Black* (Mr. Mason).
1. P. to K. 4th.	1. P. to K. 4th.
2. Kt. to K. B. 3d.	2. Kt. to Q. B. 3d.
3. B. to Q. Kt. 5th.	3. Kt. to K. B. 3d.
4. Castles. (*a*)	4. P. to Q. 3d (*b*)
5. Q. Kt. to B. 3d. (*c*)	5. B. to K. 2d.
6. P. to Q. 4th.	6. B. to Q. 2d.
7. P. to Q. 5th.	7. Q. Kt. to Kt. sq.
8. B. to Q. 3d.	8. Castles.
9. P. to K. R. 3d. (*d*)	9. P. to Q. R. 3d. (*e*)
10. Kt. to R. 2d.	10. P. to Q. B. 4th.
11. P. to K. B. 4th.	11. P. to Q. Kt. 4th.
12. P. to Q. Kt. 3d.	12. Q. to Q. Kt. 3d. (*f*)
13. Q. to K. sq.	13. P. to Q. Kt. 5th.
14. Q. Kt. to Q. sq.	14. B. to Q. Kt. 4th.
15. P. x P.	15. P. x P.
16. K. to R. sq.	16. Q. Kt. to Q. 2d.
17. Kt. to K. 3d.	17. Kt. to K. sq.
18. Kt. to K. B. 5th.	18. B. to Q. sq.
19. P. to Q. R. 3d.	19. B. x B.
20. P. x B.	20. P. x P.
21. R. x P.	21. P. to Q. R. 4th.

White (Mr. Barbour).	*Black* (Mr. Mason).
22. B. to Q. 2d.	22. R. to Q. R. 3d.
23. Kt. to K. B. 3d.	23. K. to R. sq.
24. B. to Q. B. 3d.	24. P. to K. B. 3d.
25. Kt. to Q. 2d.	25. Q. to Q. Kt. 4th.
26. Kt. to Q. B. 4th. (*g*)	26. P. to K. Kt. 3d.
27. Kt. fr. B. 5th to K. 3d.	27. Kt. to K. Kt. 2d.
28. P. to K. Kt. 4th. (*h*)	28. K. to Kt. sq.
29. Q. to Q. sq.	29. Kt. to K. sq.
30. R. to K. B. 2d.	30. Kt. to Q. 3d. (*i*)
31. Kt. x Kt.	31. R. x Kt.
32. Kt. to Q. B. 4th.	32. R. to Q. R. 3d.
33. K. R. to Q. R. 2d.	33. B. to B. 2d.
34. B. x P.	34. B. x B.
35. R. x B.	35. R. x R.
36. R. x R.	36. Q. to Kt. 2d.
37. Q. to Q. B. 2d.	37. R. to Kt. sq.
38. Kt. to Q. 2d.	38. P. to K. B. 4th. (*j*)
39. Kt. P. x P.	39. P. x P.
40. R. to R. sq.	40. P. to K. B. 5th.
41. R. to Kt. sq., check.	41. K. to R. sq.
42. Kt. to Q. B. 4th.	42. Q. to R. 3d. (*k*)
43. Q. to Q. Kt. 2d. (*l*)	43. Q. to K. B. 3d.
44. Q. to K. Kt. 2d.	44. R. to K. B. sq.
45. Q. to K. Kt. 5th. (*m*)	45. P. to K. R. 3d.
46. Q. x Q.	46. R. x Q.
47. K. to Kt. 2d.	47. R. to Q. R. 3d.
48. K. to B. 3d.	48. K. to R. 2d.
49. P. to R. 4th.	49. R. to Q. R. 7th.
50. K. to Kt. 4th.	50. K. to Kt. 3d.
51. K. to R. 3d., dis. check.	51. K. to R. 2d.
52. P. to R. 5th.	52. R. to K. B. 7th.
53. K. to K. Kt. 4th.	53. R. to K. R. 7th.

White (Mr. Barbour).	*Black* (Mr. Mason).
54. K. to K. B. 5th. (*n*)	54. R. x P., check.
55. K. to K. 6th.	55. Kt. to B. sq., check.
56. K. to B. 7th.	56. Kt. to Q. 2d.
57. K. to K. 7th.	57. Kt. to Kt. sq.
58. K. to Q. 6th.	58. R. to R. 7th.
59. Kt. x P.	59. R. to Q. Kt. 7th.
60. K. x P.	60. R. x P.
61. R. to K. B. sq.	61. Kt. to R. 3d, check.
62. K. to B. 4th.	62. R. to Kt. 5th, check.
63. K. to B. 3d. (*o*)	63. R. to Kt. 3d.
64. R. x P.	64. P. to R. 4th.
65. R. to R. 4th.	65. K. to R. 3d.
66. Kt. to B. 3d.	66. Kt. to B. 4th.
67. K. to Q. 4th.	67. Kt. to Q. 2d.
68. R. to B. 4th.	68. R. to Kt. 5th, check.
69. K. to K. 3d.	69. R. to Kt. 4th.
70. R. to B. 7th.	70. Kt. to Kt. 3d.
71. R. to B. 6th, check.	71. K. to Kt. 2d.
72. R. to Q. B. 6th.	72. Kt. x P., check. (*p*)
73. P. x Kt.	73. R. x P.
74. K. to K. 4th.	74. R. to Q. sq.
75. Kt. to K. 5th.	75. R. to B. sq.
76. R. to Kt. 6th, check.	76. K. to R. 2d.
77. R. to Kt. 5th.	77. K. to R. 3d.
78. R. to Kt. 2d.	78. P. to K. R. 5th. (*q*)
79. R. to Kt. 4th.	79. K. to R. 4th.
80. R. x P., check.	80. K. to Kt. 4th.
81. R. to Kt. 4th, check.	81. K. to R. 4th.
82. R. to Kt. 7th.	82. K. to R. 3d.
83. R. to Kt. sq.	83. R. to Q. Kt. sq.
84. P. to Q. 4th.	84. R. to Kt. 5th.
85. Kt. to B. 7th, check.	85. K. to R. 2d.

White (Mr. Barbour).	*Black* (Mr. Mason).
86. K. to K. 5th.	86. R. to Kt. 4th, check.
87. P. to Q. 5th. (*r*)	87. R. x P., check.
88. K. to B. 6th.	88. R. to B. 4th, check.
89. K. to K. 7th.	89. R. to Q. R. 4th. (*s*)
90. R. to R. sq., check.	90. K. to Kt. 2d.
91. R. to Kt. sq., check.	91. K. to R. 2d.

And the game was abandoned as drawn.

NOTES BY W. H. SAYEN.

(*a*) P. to Q. 4th we think gives the stronger attack.

(*b*) Kt. x K. P. is the correct play.

(*c*) P. to Q. 4th would have resulted in a better position, *i.e.* :—

5. P. to Q. 4th.	5. B. to Q. 2d, best.
6. P. to Q. 5th.	6. Kt. to Kt. sq.
7. B. to Q. 3d.	

With the best game, as he follows with 8. P. to Q. Kt. 3d, 9. P. to Q. B. 4th, and 10. B. to Kt. 2d.

(*d*) A good move, as it limits the action of the Q. B. of Black, and also enables White to place Kt. at R. 2, and throw forward the K. B. P.

(*e*) The only plan for Black to free his game is to throw forward his Queen's Pawns, but, in the effort, they became weak, and eventually one was lost.

(*f*) We think we would have preferred keeping the Queen at home, where she could, in the future, be used advantageously on either side, and, instead of the move in the text, have played 12. P. to K. Kt. 3d, threatening Kt. to K. R. 4th and Kt. 6th.

(*g*) Mr. Barbour's handling of his Knights in this game is worthy of deep study. The Q. R. P. must eventually fall.

(*h*) An excellent precautionary move to avoid any trouble occasioned by Kt. to R. 4th. It also threatens P. to Kt. 5th, which might prove serious.

(*i*) He has nothing better, for, play as he may, he cannot save the Q. R. P.

(*j*) Very risky, yet his game is virtually lost.

(*k*) If 42. Q. x Kt. P., White mates in two moves by 43. Q. to K. Kt. 2d.

(*l*) 44. Q. to K. Kt. 2d at once was better play, *i.e.* :—

44. Q. to K. Kt. 2d.	44. Q. to K. B. 3d.
45. Q. to Kt. 4th.	45. R. to Q. sq.
46. Q. to K. 6th.	46. Q. x Q.
47. P. x Q.	47. P. to K. R. 3d, best.
48. P. x Kt., and wines.	

(*m*) Even here White might have played 45. Q. to K. Kt. 4th, when the following might have resulted :—

45. Q. to K. Kt. 4th.	45. Kt. to Kt. sq.
46. Q. to K. 6th.	46. Q. x Q.
47. P. x Q.	47. R. to K. sq.
48. Kt. x K. P.	48. P. to K. R. 3d.
49. R. to Kt. 6th.	49. K. to R. 2d.
50. R. to B. 6th.	50. K. to Kt. 2d.
51. R. to B. 7th, check.	51. K. to Kt. sq., best.
52. Kt. to Q. 7th.	52. Kt. x Kt.
53. P. x Kt.	53. K. x R.
54. P. x R. Queens.	54. K. x Q.
55. K. to Kt. 2d, and wins.	

(*n*) Very well played. He wins the K. P. and Q. B. P. by force.

(*o*) We think 62. K. to Q. 6th would have won more easily. Mr. Barbour, however, played this part of the game with a care, which, had he exercised it later, would have given him credit.

(*p*) With the faint hope of a draw, which was, fortunately, afterwards accomplished.

(*q*) Black walked into the trap at once. He now loses a Pawn. Mr. Mason moved carelessly at this point of the game.

(*r*) An unfortunate oversight, which enables Black to draw a hard-earned victory.

(*s*) R. to B. 7th would have lost the game, White answering 90. K. to B. 8th.

GAME No. 17.

Played on August 19th, 1876, commencing at 2 P. M.

TIME, 4 HOURS.

French Defence.

White (Mr. Roberts).	*Black* (Mr. Elson).
1. P. to K. 4th.	1. P. to K. 3d.
2. P. to Q. 4th.	2. P. to Q. 4th.
3. Kt. to Q. B. 3d.	3. B. to Q. Kt. 5th.
4. P. x P.	4. P. x P.
5. Kt. to K. B. 3d.	5. Kt. to K. B. 3d.
6. B. to Q. 3d.	6. Castles.
7. Castles.	7. P. to K. R. 3d.
8. Kt. to K. 2d.	8. B. to Q. 3d.
9. B. to K. 3d.	9. Kt. to Q. B. 3d.
10. P. to Q. B. 3d.	10. B. to K. 3d.
11. Q. to B. (*a*)	11. Kt. to K. 5th. (*b*)
12. K. Kt. to Q. 2d.	12. Kt. x Kt.
13. Q. x Kt.	13. Q. to K. R. 5th.
14. P. to K. B. 4th.	14. P. to K. B. 4th.
15. R. to B. 3d.	15. Q. R. to K. sq.
16. Q. R. to K. B. sq.	16. Kt. to Kt. sq. (*c*)
17. R. to K. R. 3d.	17. Q. to K. 2d.
18. Q. R. to K. B. 3d.	18. Kt. to Q. 2d.
19. Kt. to Kt. 3d.	19. K. to R. 2d,
20. Q. to Q. B. 2d.	20. P. to K. Kt. 3d,
21. B. to B. 2d.	21. P. to Q. B. 3d.

White (Mr. Roberts).	*Black* (Mr. Elson).
22. Kt. to K. 2d.	22. Q. to B. 2d.
23. B. to R. 4th.	23. K. to Kt. 2d. (*d*)
24. K. to R. sq.	24. B. to K. 2d.
25. Q. to B. sq.	25. B. x B.
26. R. x B.	26. Kt. to K. B. 3d.
27. R. to K. B. sq.	27. P. to K. R. 4th.
28. Q. to K. sq.	28. Kt. to K. 5th.
29. P. to Q. Kt. 3d.	29. Q. to K. B. 3d.
30. R. to R. 3d.	30. B. to B. sq.
31. Q. to B. sq.	31. R. to K. 2d.
32. Kt. to Kt. 3d. (*e*)	32. K. to B. 2d.
33. K. to Kt.	33. R. from B. to K. sq.
34. R. to K. sq.	34. Kt. x Kt.
35. R. x R., check.	35. Q. x R.
36. R. x Kt.	36. Q. to K. 8th, check.
37. Q. x Q.	37. R. x Q., check.
38. K. to B. 2d.	38. R. to R. 8th. (*f*)

And the game was finally drawn.

NOTES BY JACOB ELSON.

(*a*) With the intention of taking off K. to R. P. at the proper moment with the B.

(*b*) The correct reply.

(*c*) With the intention of bringing this Kt. to Q. 2d, B. 3d, and finally K. 5th.

(*d*) Had Black played B. to K. 2d at once, White would have replied B. to Kt. 5th.

(*e*) Threatening to take off the Kt. with B., and afterwards the R. P. with the Rook, which Black could not retake without losing his Queen.

(*f*) Black won the R. P., but did not have sufficient advantage in the end to win.

GAME No. 18.

Played on August 19th, 1876, commencing at 9 A. M.

TIME, 1 HOUR 45 MINUTES.

Sicilian Defence.

White (MR. MASON).	*Black* (MR. BARBOUR).
1. P. to K. 4th.	1. P. to K. 3d.
2. P. to Q. 4th.	2. P. to Q. B. 4th.
3. Kt. to K. B. 3d.	3. P. x P.
4. Kt. x P.	4. P. to Q. R. 3d. (*a*)
5. B. to Q. 3d.	5. P. to K. 4th.
6. Kt. to K. B. 3d.	6. Kt. to Q. B. 3d.
7. Castles.	7. P. to Q. 3d.
8. Kt. to Q. B. 3d.	8. B. to K. Kt. 5th.
9. Kt. to Q. 5th.	9. Kt. to Q. 5th.
10. B. to K. 2d.	10. Kt. x B., check.
11. Q. x Kt.	11. Kt. to K. 2d.
12. Kt. to K. 3d.	12. B. to Q. 2d.
13. P. to Q. Kt. 3d.	13. P. to K. Kt. 3d.
14. B. to R. 3d.	14. Kt. to Q. B. sq.
15. K. R. to Q. sq.	15. Q. to R. 4th.
16. B. to Kt. 2d.	16. P. to Q. Kt. 4th.
17. Q. to Q. 3d.	17. B. to K. Kt. 2d. (*b*)
18. B. x P.	18. B. x B.
19. Kt. x B.	19. Q. to Q. sq.
20. Kt. x B.	20. Q. x Kt.
21. Kt. to Q. 5th.	21. Q. to Q. sq.

White (Mr. Mason).	*Black* (Mr. Barbour).
22. Q. to Q. 4th.	22. K. to Q. 2d.
23. P. to Q. B. 4th.	23. R. to B. sq.
24. P. to Q. B. 5th.	24. P. to K. B. 3d.
25. P. x P.	25. Q. R. to Kt. sq.
26. Q. R. to B. sq.	26. K. to K. 3d.

27. Kt. to Q. B. 7th, check, and Mr. Barbour resigned.

NOTES BY W. H. SAYEN.

(*a*) Much better Kt. to K. B. 3d.

(*b*) An oversight, caused by misapprehension.

GAME No. 19.

Played on August 19th, 1876, commencing at 11 A.M.

TIME, 4 HOURS 30 MINUTES.

Stein Opening.

White (MR. MARTINEZ).	*Black* (MR. MASON).
1. P. to Q. 4th.	1. P. to K. B. 4th.
2. P. to K. 4th (*a*)	2. P. x P.
3. Kt. to Q. B. 3d.	3. Kt. to K. B. 3d.
4. B. to K. Kt. 5th.	4. P. to Q. B. 3d. (*b*)
5. P. to K. B. 3d. (*c*)	5. P. x P.
6. Kt. x P.	6. P. to Q. 3d. (*d*)
7. B. to Q. 3d.	7. B. to K. Kt. 5th.
8. Castles.	8. Q. Kt. to Q. 2d.
9. P. to K. R. 3d.	9. B. x Kt.
10. R. x B.	10. Q. to Kt. 3d.
11. K. to R. sq.	11. Castles. (*e*)
12. B. to K. B. 5th.	12. P. to K. Kt. 3d.
13. B. x K. Kt. (*f*)	13. P. x B.
14. B. to K. 6th.	14. P. to K. B. 4th.
15. Kt. to K. 2d. (*g*)	15. P. to Q. 4th.
16. P. to Q. B. 4th.	16. P. x P.
17. B. x P.	17. Kt. to K. B. 3d.
18. R. to Q. Kt. 3d.	18. Q. to R. 4th.
19. R. to Q. B.	19. Kt. to K. 5th. (*h*)
20. Q. to B. 2d. (*i*)	20. K. to Kt.
21. B. to Q. 3d.	21. Kt. to B. 7th.

White (Mr. Martinez).	*Black* (Mr. Mason).
22. K. to Kt.	22. Kt. x B.
23. Q. x Kt.	23. B. to Q. 3d.
24. Q. to B. 4th.	24. K. to R.
25. Q. to K. B. 7th.	25. Q. to B. 2d.
26. Q. to Q. B. 4th.	26. K. R. to K. sq.
27. Q. R. to Q. sq.	27. Q. to K. 2d.
28. K. to B. sq.	28. Q. to K. 5th.
29. P. to Q. R. 4th.	29. R. to K. 2d.
30. P. to R. 5th.	30. Q. R. to K.
31. R. to K.	31. P. to Q. R. 3d.
32. R. to Q. 3d.	32. P. to K. Kt. 4th.
33. Q. to B. 3d.	33. P. to K. Kt. 5th.
34. K. R. to Q.	34. P. to R. 4th.
35. P. to Q. Kt. 3d.	35. P. to K. R. 5th.
36. K. to Kt.	36. Q. to K. 6th, check.
37. K. to B.	37. P. x P.
38. P. x P.	38. B. to Q. Kt. 5th. (*j*)
39. Q. x Q.	39. R. x Q.
40. K. to B. 2d.	40. B. x R., check.
41. R. x B.	41. P. to K. B. 5th.
42. R. to Q.	42. R. x Kt., check.

And Black won the game.

NOTES BY W. H. SAYEN.

(*a*) This sacrifice of the Pawn cannot be considered theoretically sound.

(*b*) The best move to prevent the regaining of the Pawn by the following advantageous line of play:—

5. B. x Kt.	5. K. P. x B.
6. Q. to R. 5th, check.	6. P. to Kt. 3d.
7. Q. to Q. 5th, with the best game.	

(*c*) White might here have regained the Pawn by B. x Kt., but would have lost all attack. This move is new, and gives a fine attack.

(*d*) Best, to prevent the posting of the Kt. at K. 5th, and also freeing Q. B.

(*e*) It is evident he cannot take the Q. P.

(*f*) Certainly here White could have gained an advantage by playing B. to K. 6th at once, and saved the valuable Q. B., which could have been retreated with advantage to K. B. 4th or K. 3d on the following move, and Black would not risk P. to Q. 4th on account of this dangerous Bishop.

(*g*) P. to Q. 5th, followed by 16. Kt. to R. 4th, and 17. P. to Q. B. 4th, would surely have been a much better line of play and less easily defensible than the one adopted.

(*h*) Black has now secured a fine position, and his own game is easily defensible, whilst the isolated Q. P. of White is marked for sacrifice.

(*i*) Again B. to K. 6th, check, followed by Q. to B. 2d, would, we think, have been stronger play.

(*j*) The "coup décisif." The game, however, has been lost for several moves back. Black finishes it neatly.

GAME No. 20.

Played on August 21st, commencing at 9 A.M.

TIME, 6 HOURS.

French Defence.

White (Mr. Mason).	*Black* (Mr. Martinez).
1. P. to K. 4th.	1. P. to K. 3d.
2. P. to Q. 4th.	2. P. to Q. 4th.
3. Kt. to Q. B. 3d. (*a*)	3. B. to Q. Kt. 5th.
4. P. x P.	4. P. x P.
5. Kt. to K. B. 3d.	5. Kt. to K. B. 3d.
6. B. to Q. 3d.	6. Castles.
7. Castles.	7. B. to Q. 3d. (*b*)
8. B. to K. Kt. 5th.	8. P. to Q. B. 3d.
9. Q. to Q. 2d.	9. B. to K. 3d.
10. Q. R. to K. sq.	10. Q. Kt. to Q. 2d.
11. Kt. to K. 2d.	11. Q. to B. 2d.
12. Kt. to Kt. 3d.	12. K. R. to K. sq.
13. B. x Kt.	13. Kt. x B.
14. Kt. to K. 5th.	14. Kt. to Q. 2d. (*c*)
15. Q. to Kt. 5th. (*d*)	15. P. to K. B. 3d. (*e*)
16. Q. to R. 5th.	16. P. x Kt. (*f*)
17. Q. x R. P., check.	17. K. to B. sq.
18. B. to Kt. 6th. (*g*)	18. B. to Kt. sq.
19. Q. to R. 8th.	19. R. to K. 3d. (*h*)
20. P. to K. B. 4th. (*i*)	20. R. x B. (*j*)

White (Mr. Mason).	*Black* (Mr. Martinez).
21. P. x P., dis. check.	21. Kt. to B. 3d.
22. P. x Kt.	22. P. x P.
23. R. x P., check.	23. R. x R.
24. Q. x R., check.	24. B. to B. 2d. (*k*)
25. Kt. to B. 5th. (*l*)	25. B. x P., check. (*m*)
26. K. to R. sq.	26. B. to K. 4th.
27. R. x B.	

And Mr. Martinez resigned. (*n*)

NOTES BY W. H. SAYEN.

(*a*) The *Handbuch* gives this as the best move, considering it stronger than P. x P., and follows it up thus:—

	3. B. to Q. Kt. 5th.
4. P. x P.	4. P. x P.
5. Kt. to K. B. 3d.	5. Kt. to K. B. 3d.
6. B. to Q. 3d.	6. Castles.
7. Castles.	7. B. to K. Kt. 5th, etc.,

and finally gives an even game.

But other authorities contend that this invention of Mr. Paulsen is not good, as the Bishop is not poorly placed.

(*b*) This move was the source of many of Black's subsequent troubles, as the Bishop here completely blocks his game, and always tempts the threatening move of P. to K. B. 4th. The correct place for this Bishop was at Q. Kt. 5th. Besides exchanging the K. B. for the Q. Kt., in a close opening, is generally always good play. B. to K. Kt. 5th, was the proper move.

(c) This was probably the best move under the circumstances, as he scarcely dared play B. x Kt., for instance—

	14. B. x Kt.
15. P. x B.	15. Kt. to Kt. 5th. (1)
16. P. to K. B. 4th.	16. Q. to Kt. 3d, check.
17. K. to R. sq.	17. P. to K. Kt. 3d, best.
18. P. to B. 5th.	18. B. to Q. 2d.
19. Q. to Kt. 5th.	19. Kt. to B. 7th, check.
20. R. x Kt.	20. Q. x R.
21. R. to K. B.	21. Q. to Q. B. 4th.
22. Kt. to R. 5th.	

And the game is forced.

(1)

	15. Kt. to Q. 2d.
16. P. to K. B. 4th.	16. Kt. to B. sq.
17. P. to B. 5th.	17. B. to Q. 2d.
18. Q. to Kt. 5th.	18. P. to K. R. 3d.
19. Q. to Kt. 4th.	19. R. x K. P.
20. Kt. to R. 5th.	20. P. to K. Kt. 4th.
21. Q. to Q. 4th, and wins.	

(*d*) A beautiful conception, and perfectly sound.

(*e*) He has nothing better than this; the only hope being to evade the attack by the sacrifice of the piece here won.

(*f*) It is self-evident he could not play P. to Kt. 3d.

(*g*) The move wanted, and played with a remarkable judgment of position.

(*h*) The only hope for Black here was P. to K. 5th, to avoid the terrible effects of White's P. to K. B. 4th, viz. :—

	19. P. to K. 5th. (1)
20. Kt. to Kt. 5th.	20. Kt. to K. B. 3d.
21. P. to K. B. 3d.	21. P. to K. 6th.
22. P. to K. R. 4th.	22. B. to B. 5th.
23. P. to K. R. 5th.	

And still Black cannot save the game.

(1)

Or if he play—

	19. Kt. to K. B. 3d.
20. Kt. to Kt. 5th.	20. P. x P., or anything.
21. P. to K. R. 4th.	21. R. x R.
22. R. x R.,	

And we do not see how Black can escape the fatal effects of the K. R. P. being pushed; for if he play B. to K. B. 5th, White answers with R. to K. 7th.

(*i*) The winning move, Black has now no resource.

(*j*) Any other move would have lost equally; take the most obvious—

	20. P. to K. 5th.
21. P. to B. 5th.	21. R. to K. 2d, best.
22. P. to B. 6th.	22. P. x P.
23. R. x P., check.	23. Kt. x R.
24. Q. x Kt., check.	24. R. to B. 2d.
25. B. x R.	25. B. x B.
26. Kt. to B. 5th, and wins.	

(*k*) He had nothing better.

(*l*) The *coup de grâce.* The game is now forced.

(*m*) Merely to prolong the game, and endeavoring to secure every chance in the event of weak play by his adversary.

(*n*) This game is truly a chess study, and was one of the gems of the Tourney.

GAME No. 21.

Played on August 21st, 1876, commencing at 9 A. M.

TIME, 4 HOURS.

Scotch Gambit.

White (Mr. Bird).	*Black* (Mr. Roberts).
1. P. to K. 4th.	1. P. to K. 4th.
2. Kt. to K. B. 3d.	2. Q. Kt. to K. B. 3d.
3. P. to Q. 4th.	3. P. x P.
4. Kt. x P.	4. Q. to R. 5th.
5. Kt. to Kt. 5th.	5. Q. x K. P., check.
6. B. to K. 3d. (*a*)	6. B. to Kt. 5th, check.
7. Q. Kt. to Q. 2d.	7. B. x Kt., check. (*b*)
8. Q. x B.	8. K. to Q. sq.
9. Castles.	9. P. to Q. R. 3d. (*c*)
10. Kt. x Q. B. P. (*d*)	10. K. x Kt.
11. Q. to Q. 6th, check.	11. K. to Q. sq.
12. Q. to B. 8th, check.	12. K. to B. 2d. (*e*)
13. Q. to Q. 6th, check.	13. K. to Q. sq.
14. B. to Kt. 6th, check.	14. K. to K. sq.
15. B. to Q. 3d.	15. Q. to K. R. 5th. (*f*)
16. K. R. to K. sq., check.	16. K. Kt. to K. 2d.
17. B. to K. 4th.	17. Q. to R. 3d, check.
18. Q. x Q.	18. Kt. P. x Q.
19. B. x Kt.	19. Kt. P. x B. (*g*)
20. B. to Q. B. 5th.	20. P. to Q. 3d.
21. R. x P.	21. B. to K. 3d. (*h*)

White (Mr. Bird).	*Black* (Mr. Roberts).
22. R. x B.	22. P. x R.
23. R. x K. P.	23. K. to B. 2d.
24. R. x Kt., check.	24. K. to B. 3d.
25. R. to Q. 7th.	25. K. R. to K. sq.
26. B. to K. 3d.	26. K. to K. 3d. (*i*)
27. R. x R. P.	27. R. to K. R. sq.
28. R. x R. P.	28. R. x R
29. B. x R.	29. K. to B. 4th.
30. B. to K. 3d.	30. K. to K. 5th.
31. P. to K. R. 4th.	31. R. to Q. sq.
32. P. to K. R. 5th.	32. R. to K. Kt. sq.
33. P. to K. Kt. 3d.	33. R. to Q. sq.
34. P. to K. R. 6th.	34. K. to B. 6th.
35. P. to Q B. 3d.	35. R. to Q. 4th.
36. P. to Q. Kt. 4th.	36. R. to Q. 2d.
37. B. to Q. 4th.	37. K. to Kt. 4th.
38. B. to Kt. 7th.	Resigns.

NOTES BY W. H. SAYEN.

(*a*) The *Handbuch* here gives B. to K. 2d, and gives Black eventually the best game.

(*b*) A very bad move. He should have played Q. to K. 4th, *i. e.*

	7. Q. to K. 4th.
8. P. to Q. B. 3d.	8. B. to R. 4th.
9. P. to Q. Kt. 4th.	9. P. to Q. R. 3d.
10. Kt. to R. 3d.	10. B. to Kt. 3d.
11. B. x B.	11. P. x B.
12. Kt. fr. R. 3d to B. 4th.	12. P. to Q Kt. 4th.
13. Kt. to K. 3d.	13. Kt. to K. 2d,

and Black retains his Pawn, with a threatening position on the King's side.

(*c*) Black seemed oblivious of the threatened danger. 9. Kt. to K. B. 3d, was the correct move here.

(*d*) Played in Mr. Bird's happiest style. This sacrifice, after careful analysis, appears to be perfectly sound.

(*e*) It is self-evident that if he interpose the Queen, mate follows at Q. Kt. 6th.

(*f*) The best and only move, in fact, if—

	15. Q. to Kt. 5th.
16. K. R. to K. sq., check.	16. K. Kt. to K. 2d.
17. R. x Kt., check.	17. Kt. x Kt.
18. Q. R. to K. sq.	18. Q. to Kt. 4th, check.
19. P. to K. B. 4th.	19. Q. to B. 3d.
20. Q. to B. 7th, and wins.	

(*g*) Another singular position. Q. P. x B. cannot be played on account of the threatened mate.

(*h*) The piece might here have been saved by the following line of play:—

	21. R. to Q. Kt. sq.
22. R. x Q. B. P.	22. R. to Kt. 2d.
23. R. x K. R. P.	23. R. to Q. 2d.

And White retains 3 Pawns for his piece, and ought to win.

(*i*) Black had here, perhaps, a chance for a draw, by playing 26. R. to K. 2d, in which case White would have retreated his Rook to Q. 2d, and finally won by the King's Pawns.

GAME No. 22.

Played on August 21st, 1876, commencing at 2 P. M.

TIME, 1 HOUR 10 MINUTES.

Ruy Lopez's Knight's Game.

White (Mr. Roberts).	*Black* (Mr. Bird).
1. P. to K. 4th.	1. P. to K. 4th.
2. Kt. to K. B. 3d.	2. Kt. to Q. B. 3d.
3. B. to Kt. 5th.	3. P. to Q. R. 3d.
4. B. to R. 4th.	4. Kt. to K. B. 3d.
5. Castles.	5. Kt. x K. P.
6. R. to K. (*a*)	6. Kt. to Q. B. 4th.
7. B. x Q. Kt.	7. Q. P. x B.
8. Kt. x K. P.	8. B. to K. 2d.
9. Q. to K. 2d. (*b*)	9. B. to K. 3d.
10. P. to Q. B. 3d.	10. Kt. to Q. 2d.
11. P. to K. B. 4th.	11. Kt. x Kt.
12. Q. x Kt. (*c*)	12. B. to K. B. 3d.
13. Q. to Q. B. 5th.	13. B. to K. 2d.
14. Q. to K. R. 5th.	14. P. to K. Kt. 3d.
15. Q. to K. 2d.	15. P. to Q. B. 4th.
16. K. to R. sq.	16. Q. to Q. 2d.
17. P. to Q. 3d. (*d*)	17. Castles, Q. R.
18. R. to Q. sq. (*e*)	18. B. to K. Kt. 5th.
19. Q. to K. sq.	19. B. x R.
20. Q. x B.	20. Q. x Q. P.

And White resigned in a few moves.

NOTES BY W. H. SAYEN.

(*a*) We consider this attack as fallacious, and entirely superficial, depending in a great measure on Black's interposition of the B. at K. 3d. We think B. to K. 2d relieves Black in a great measure, and he need not then fear the threatened move of Q. to K. R. 5th. We think 6. P. to Q. 4th is much stronger for White, *i. e.*:—

6. P. to Q. 4th.	6. P. to Q. Kt. 4th.
7. B. to Kt. 3d.	7. P. to Q. 4th.
8. Q. P. x K. P.	8. B. to K. 3d.
9. B. to K. 3d.	9. B. to K. 2d.

10. Q. to K. 2d, and we prefer the White game, as the Black Queen's Pawns are necessarily weak.

(*b*) Very weak play. P. to Q. 3d, followed by Kt. to Q. B. 3d, and later P. to K. B. 4th, would have been much better.

(*c*) We certainly prefer B. P. x Kt.

(*d*) He should first have played 17. P. to K. R. 3d.

(*e*) A fatal blunder. He could not save the Pawn. Better Q. to K. B. 2d, followed by B. to K. 3d.

GAME No. 23.

Played on August 21st, 1876, commencing at 9 A.M.

TIME, 3 HOURS.

Petroff's Defence.

White (Mr. Barbour).	*Black* (Mr. Davidson).
1. P. to K. 4th.	1. P. to K. 4th.
2. Kt. to K. B. 3d.	2. Kt. to K. B. 3d.
3. P. to Q. 4th.	3. Kt. x P.
4. B. to Q. 3d.	4. P. to Q. 4th.
5. Kt. x P.	5. B. to K. 2d.
6. Castles.	6. Castles.
7. P. to Q. B. 4th.	7. Kt. to K. B. 3d.
8. P. to B. 5th. (*a*)	8. Kt. to Q. B. 3d.
9. Kt. x Kt.	9. P. x Kt.
10. Kt. to Q. B. 3d.	10. R. to Kt.
11. P. to Q. R. 3d.	11. B. to Kt. 5th.
12. P. to B. 3d.	12. B. to R. 4th.
13. Kt. to K. 2d.	13. Q. to Q. 2d.
14. P. to Q. Kt. 4th.	14. K. to R. sq.
15. B. to Q. 2d.	15. Kt. to Kt. sq.
16. Kt. to Kt. 3d.	16. B. to Kt. 3d.
17. Q. to B. 2d.	17. B. to B. 3d. (*b*)
18. B. to B. 3d.	18. Q. R. to K.
19. P. to B. 4th.	19. B. x B.
20. Q. x B.	20. Kt. to R. 3d.
21. Kt. to R. 5th.	21. B. to R. 5th.

White (Mr. Barbour).	*Black* (Mr. Davidson).
22. P. to Kt. 3d. (*c*)	22. B. to Q. sq.
23. P. to B. 5th. (*d*)	23. B. to Kt. 4th.
24. Q. R. to K. sq. (*e*)	24. R. x R.
25. R. x R.	25. Q. x P.
26. Q. x Q.	26. Kt. x Q.
27. R. to K. 5th.	27. P. to Kt. 3d.
28. P. to Kt. 4th.	28. P. to B. 3d.
29. R. to K. 6th.	29. Kt. to K. 6th.
30. P. to K. R. 4th.	30. Kt. x P.
31. P. x B.	31. P. x Kt.
32. B. to Q. 2d.	32. P. to K. R. 5th.
33. B. to B. 4th.	33. P. x P.
34. B. x P.	34. P. to R. 6th.
35. B. to R. 4th.	35. R. to B. 6th.
36. P. to R. 4th.	36. K. to Kt. 2d.
37. P. to Kt. 5th.	37. P. x P.
38. P. x P.	38. R. to Q. Kt. 6th.
39. P. to Kt. 6th.	39. R. P. x P.
40. P. to B. 6th.	40. R. to Kt. 8th, check.
41. R. to K. sq.	41. R. x R., check.
42. B. x R.	42. K. to B. 3d.
43. B. to Kt. 3d.	43. K. to K. 3d.
44. B. x P.	44. P. to Kt. 4th.
45. B. to Q. 8th.	45. K. to Q. 3d, and wins.

NOTES BY B. M. NEILL.

(*a*) 8. Kt. to Q. B. 3d gives White the better game. The move in the text weakens White's Q. P.

(*b*) Proper commencing an attack on Q. P.

(*c*) R. to B. 3d we think preferable.

(*d*) Black's next move proves this to be very wea)

(*e*) This gives up a P., but there seems to be no better move, If 24. R. to B. 3d, Black replies R. to K. 5th.

GAME No. 24.

Played on August 21st, 1876, commencing at 2 P. M.

TIME, 1 HOUR 45 MINUTES.

Petroff's Defence.

White (MR. DAVIDSON).	*Black* (MR. BARBOUR).
1. P. to K. 4th.	1. P. to K. 4th.
2. K. Kt. to B. 3d.	2. K. Kt. to B. 3d.
3. B. to B. 4th.	3. B. to B. 4th.
4. Kt. x P.	4. Castles.
5. P. to Q. 3d.	5. P. to Q. 4th.
6. P. x P.	6. R. to K.
7. P. to K. B. 4th.	7. Kt. to Kt. 5th.
8. P. to Q. 4th.	8. B. to Kt. 3d.
9. Castles.	9. Kt. x Kt.
10. P. x Kt.	10. R. x P.
11. P. to Q. B. 3d.	11. R. to B. 4th.
12. B. to B. 4th.	12. Q. to B. 3d.
13. B. to K. 5th.	13. Q. x B.
14. R. to K. sq.	14. Kt. to Q. 2d.
15. R. x Q.	15. Kt. x R.

And White won.

Each player's 13th move was a glaring oversight.

GAME No. 25.

Played on August 21st, 1876, commencing at 9 A. M.

TIME, 6 HOURS.

Irregular Opening.

White (Mr. Judd).	*Black* (Mr. Ware).
1. P. to K. 4th.	1. P. to Q. 4th. (*a*)
2. P. x P.	2. Q. x P.
3. Q. Kt. to B. 3d.	3. Q. to Q. sq.
4. P. to Q. 4th.	4. P. to Q. B. 3d.
5. K. Kt. to B. 3d.	5. Q. B. to B. 4th.
6. K. B. to B. 4th.	6. P. to K. 3d.
7. Castles.	7. K. Kt. to B. 3d.
8. K. Kt. to R. 4th. (*b*)	8. B. to Kt. 3d.
9. Q. B. to Kt. 5th.	9. B. to K. 2d.
10. P. to K. B. 4th. (*c*)	10. B. x B. P.
11. Q. to Q. 2d.	11. B. to Kt. 3d. (*d*)
12. P. to B. 5th. (*e*)	12. P. x P.
13. Q. R. to K. sq.	13. Castles.
14. Kt. x P.	14. B. x Kt.
15. R. x B.	15. P. to Q. Kt. 4th.
16. B. to Q. Kt. 3d.	16. Q. Kt. to Q. 2d.
17. B. to Q. B. 2d.	17. R. to K. sq.
18. Q. to Q. 3d.	18. P. to K. Kt. 3d.
19. K. R. to B. sq.	19. Kt. to R. 4th.
20. B. to Q. Kt. 3d.	20. B. to B. 3d.
21. R. x R., check.	21. Q. x R.
22. P. to K. Kt. 4th.	22. K. to R. sq.

White (Mr. Judd).	*Black* (Mr. Ware).
23. B. x B.	23. K. Kt. x B.
24. P. to Kt. 5th.	24. Kt. to Kt. 5th.
25. R. x B. P.	25. Q. to K. 8th, check. (*f*)
26. R. to B. sq.	26. Q. to K. 6th, check.
27. Q. x Q.	27. Kt. x Q.
28. R. to B. 7th.	28. R. to K. B.
29. K. to B. 2d.	29. R. x R., check.
30. B. x R.	30. Kt. to K. B. 4th.
31. B. to K. 6th.	31. Kt. to Q. Kt. 3d.
32. B. x Kt.	32. P. x B.
33. K. to B. 3d.	33. K. to Kt. 2d.
34. P. to K. R. 4th.	34. K. to Kt. 3d.
35. Kt. to K. 2d.	35. P. to Q. R. 4th.
36. Kt. to B. 4th, check.	36. K. to B. 2d.
37. P. to R. 5th.	37. P. to R. 5th.
38. Kt. to Q. 3d.	38. K. to K. 3d.
39. Kt. to Kt. 4th.	39. Kt. to B. 5th.
40. Kt. x P.	40. Kt. x P.
41. P. to Q. 5th, check. (*g*)	41. K. x P.
42. P. to Kt. 6th.	42. P. x P.
43. P. to R. 6th, and wins.	

NOTES BY B. M. NEILL.

(*a*) Inferior, and containing the seeds of defeat.

(*b*) We prefer Kt. to K. 2d.

(*c*) No doubt an oversight, but in any case we prefer Black's game.

(*d*) P. to K. R. 3d gives Black a great superiority.

(*e*) The proper style.

(*f*) In order to force the withdrawal of White's R. from its present strong position.

(*g*) Mr. Judd plays the ending admirably.

GAME No. 26.

Played on August 22d, 1876, commencing at 9 A.M.

TIME, 2 HOURS.

Ruy Lopez's Knight's Game.

White (MR. MASON).	*Black* (MR. ROBERTS).
1. P. to K. 4th.	1. P. to K. 4th.
2. Kt. to K. B. 3d.	2. Kt. to Q. B. 3d.
3. B. to Kt. 5th.	3. P. to Q. R. 3d.
4. B. to R. 4th.	4. Kt. to B. 3d.
5. Q. to K. 2d. (*a*)	5. P. to Q. Kt. 4th.
6. B. to Kt. 3d.	6. B. to Kt. 2d.
7. P. to Q. B. 3d.	7. B. to B. 4th.
8. P. to Q. 3d.	8. P. to Q. 3d.
9. Castles.	9. Castles. (*b*)
10. B. to K. Kt. 5th.	10. K. to R. sq.
11. Q. Kt. to Q. 2d.	11. Q. to Q. 2d. (*c*)
12. B. x Kt.	12. P. x B.
13. Kt. to R. 4th.	13. R. to K. Kt. sq.
14. Q. to R. 5th.	14. Kt. to Q. sq.
15. Q. to R. 6th.	15. Q. to Kt. 5th. (*d*)
16. Q. x B. P., check.	16. R. to Kt. 2d.
17. Q. Kt. to K. B. 3d.	17. Kt. to K. 3d.
18. B. x Kt.	18. P. x B.
19. P. to K. R. 3d.	19. Q. to R. 4th.
20. K. to R. 2d.	20. P. to Q. 4th.
21. P. to K. Kt. 4th.	21. Q. to K. sq.

White (Mr. Mason).	*Black* (Mr. Roberts).
22. Q. R. to K. sq.	22. Q. to K. Kt. sq.
23. Q. Kt. x K. P.	23. B. to K. 2d. (*e*)
24. K. Kt. to Kt. 6th, ch.	24. P. x Kt.
25. Kt. x P., check.	25. K. to R. 2d.
26. Kt. x B.	26. R. x Kt.
27. Q. x R., check.	27. Q. to Kt. 2d.
28. Q. x Q., check.	28. K. x Q.

And Mr. Roberts resigned.

NOTES BY W. H. SAYEN.

(*a*) Steinitz and many English authorities consider this the best attack.

(*b*) We should first have played P. to K. R. 3d.

(*c*) Bad play. Better P. to K. R. 3d.

(*d*) He could not save the Pawn without getting a losing position at once.

(*e*) Better B. to Q. 3d. This loses at once, though the game was virtually gone.

GAME No. 27.

Played on August 22d, 1876, commencing at 2 P. M.

TIME, 2 HOURS.

Petroff's Defence.

White (MR. ROBERTS).	*Black* (MR. MASON).
1. P. to K. 4th.	1. P. to K. 4th.
2. Kt. to K. B. 3d.	2. Kt. to K. B. 3d.
3. P. to Q. 4th. (*a*)	3. Kt. x P. (*b*)
4. B. to Q. 3d.	4. P. to Q. 4th.
5. Kt. x P.	5. B. to K. 2d. (*c*)
6. Castles.	6. Castles.
7. P. to Q. B. 4th.	7. Kt. to K. B. 3d.
8. Q. to Kt. 3d.	8. P. to Q. B. 3d. (*d*)
9. Kt. to Q. B. 3d.	9. P. to Q. Kt. 3d.
10. R. to K. sq.	10. B. to Kt. 2d.
11. B. to K. Kt. 5th.	11. Q. Kt. to Q. 2d.
12. B. to B. 5th.	12. Kt. x Kt.
13. P. x Kt.	13. Kt. to Q. 2d.
14. B. x B.	14. Q. x B.
15. P. x P. (*e*)	15. Kt. x P.
16. Q. R. to Q. sq.	16. P. x P.
17. Kt. x P.	17. B. x Kt.
18. Q. x B. (*f*)	18. Q. R. to Q. sq.
19. Q. to K. 4th.	19. P. to Kt. 3d.
20. B. to Q. 7th.	20. R. x B.
21. R. x R.	21. Q. x R.

And the game was drawn.

NOTES BY W. H. SAYEN.

(*a*) Many authorities prefer this form of attack, as giving White the best game; we, however, prefer 3. Kt. x K. P. as more satisfactory.

(*b*) Much better than P. x P.

(*c*) We now have the first position.

(*d*) Here we much prefer Q. Kt. to Q. 2d, *i. e.*—

	8. Q. Kt. to Q. 2d.
9. P. x P.	9. Q. Kt. to Kt. 3d.,

and regains the Pawn, with a good game.

(*e*) We here would have preferred 15. B. x Kt.

(*f*) If R. x B. it is evident Black wins by Kt. to B. 6th, check.

GAME No. 28.

Played on August 22d, 1876, commencing at 9 A. M.

TIME, 9 HOURS 15 MINUTES.

Irregular Opening.

White (Mr. Ware).	*Black* (Mr. Judd).
1. P. to Q. 4th.	1. P. to Q. 4th.
2. P. to K. B. 4th.	2. P. to K. 3d.
3. Kt. to K. B. 3d.	3. Kt. to K. B. 3d.
4. P. to K. 3d.	4. P. to Q. B. 4th. (*a*)
5. P. to Q. B. 3d.	5. Q. Kt. to B. 3d.
6. B. to Q. Kt. 5th.	6. B. to Q. 2d.
7. Castles.	7. B. to K. 2d.
8. P. to Q. R. 3d.	8. Castles.
9. B. to Q. 3d. (*b*)	9. R. to Q. B. sq.
10. P. to K. R. 3d.	10. Kt. to K. 5th.
11. Q. Kt. to Q. 2d.	11. P. to K. B. 4th. (*c*)
12. Kt. to K. 5th.	12. B. to K. sq.
13. B. to K. 2d.	13. Kt. to Kt. 6th.
14. R. to B. 2d.	14. B. to R. 5th.
15. K. Kt. to B. 3d.	15. Kt. x B., check. (*d*)
16. R. x Kt.	16. B. to K. 2d.
17. Kt. to B. sq.	17. P. to B. 5th.
18. B. to Q. 2d.	18. Kt. to R. 4th.
19. Q. to K. sq.	19. Kt. to Kt. 6th.
20. R. to Kt. sq.	20. B. to K. R. 4th.
21. Q. Kt. to R. 2d.	21. B. to R. 5th.

White (Mr. Ware).	*Black* (Mr. Judd).
22. Q. to K. B. sq.	22. Kt. x B.
23. R. x Kt.	23. B. to K. 2d.
24. P. to K. Kt. 4th. (*e*)	24. P. x P.
25. P. x P.	25. B. to Kt. 3d.
26. Q. R. to Q. sq.	26. B. to K. 5th.
27. P. to Kt. 5th.	27. Q. to K. sq.
28. Q. to R. 3d.	28. B. to K. B. 4th.
29. Q. to Kt. 3d.	29. R. to Q. B. 2d.
30. Kt. to K. 5th.	30. B. to Q. 3d.
31. Q. Kt. to B. 3d.	31. B. to K. 5th.
32. R. to R. 2d.	32. P. to Q. R. 4th.
33. Q. R. to Q. 2d.	33. P. to Q. Kt. 4th.
34. R. to R. 4th.	34. Q. B. x Kt.
35. Q. x B.	35. B. x Kt.
36. Q. P. x B.	36. R. to Q. 2d.
37. Q. to R. 3d. (*f*)	37. P. to Kt. 3d.
38. Q. to Kt. 4th.	38. K. R. to B. 2d.
39. Q. to Q. sq.	39. Q. to Q. Kt. sq.
40. Q. to B. 2d.	40. Q. to Kt. 3d.
41. K. to B. 2d.	41. P. to Kt. 5th.
42. B. P. x P.	42. R. P. x P.
43. K. to B. 3d.	43. P. to Kt. 6th. (*g*)
44. Q. to B. 3d.	44. K. to B. sq.
45. R. to K. R. sq.	45. Q. to Q. sq.
46. K. to K. 2d. (*h*)	46. Q. to Q. R. sq.
47. R. to R. 2d.	47. Q. to R. 2d.
48. K. to B. 3d.	48. K. to K. sq.
49. R. to Q. 4th.	49. Q. to B. 4th.
50. R. from R. 2d to Q 2d.	50. Q. to K. 2d.
51. R. to Kt. 2d.	51. Q. to B. sq.
52. Q. to R. 5th.	52. R. from B. 2d to K. 2d.
53. R. to R. 2d.	53. Q. to B. 2d.

White (Mr. Ware).	*Black* (Mr. Judd).
54. Q. to B. 3d.	54. Q. to B. 4th.
55. K. to Kt. 3d.	55. Q. to Kt. 8th.
56. Q. to Q. 2d.	56. R. to K. B. 2d.
57. R. to Kt. 2d.	57. Q. to B. 4th.
58. R. to R. 2d.	58. R. from B. 2d to K. 2d.
59. R. to R. sq.	59. Q. to B. 2d. (*i*)
60. K. to B. 3d.	60. R. to Kt. 2d.
61. K. to Kt. 3d.	61. R. from K. 2d to Q. 2d.
62. Q. to B. 3d.	62. Q. to B. 4th.
63. P. to K. 4th. (*j*)	63. P. x P.
64. Q. x B. P.	64. R. x R.
65. Q. x R.	65. R. to Q. 2d.
66. Q. to R. 4th. (*k*)	66. P. to K. R. 4th. (*l*)
67. P. x P. en pass. (*m*)	67. P. to K. Kt. 4th.
68. R. to K. B. sq. (*n*)	68. K. to K. 2d.
69. Q. to Kt. 4th, check.	69. K. to B. 2d.
70. K. to B. 2d. (*o*)	70. P. x P.
71. R. to K. Kt. sq.	71. P. to K. 6th, check.
72. K. to B. 3d.	72. Q. to R. 6th, check.
73. K. to K. 4th.	73. Q. x R. P.
74. R. to Kt. 4th.	74. Q. to R. 8th, check.
75. K. x P.	75. P. to K. 7th.
76. K. to Kt. 5th.	76. K. to Kt. 2d.
77. K. to B. 4th, dis. ch.	77. K. to R. 2d.

And Mr. Ware resigned.

NOTES BY W. H. SAYEN.

(*a*) The positions of Black's Pawns are certainly much superior to those of White.

(*b*) We would prefer 9. B. x Kt., followed by Kt. to K. 5th.

(*c*) Weak play. Better advance Pawns on the Q. Kt. side, after first exchanging Knights.

(*d*) B. to K. R. 4th, looks to us to be a remarkably good move, as Kt. can take Bishop, and then the K. B. be planted at Kt. 6th, and if 16. Kt. x B., Black wins the exchange.

(*e*) Dangerous play at this juncture.

(*f*) The game looks like a draw, though all the advantage of position is with White.

(*g*) P. x R. P., followed by Q. to R. 4th, and R. to R. 2d, would have probably won a Pawn.

(*h*) We would prefer Q. to Q. 4th, and force a draw.

(*i*) The game is so manifestly drawn, and it is so evident that neither can hope for victory except through an error of the adversary, that it seems silly to continue the game.

(*j*) Bad play, which ultimately loses the game.

(*k*) We consider this position a lost game for White in every variation.

(*l*) Well played.

(*m*) He had nothing better.

(*n*) The only hope was P. to K. R. 7th, and, we think, White could have drawn, *i. e.*—

68. P. to R. 7th.	68. Q. x B. P., check.
69. K. to Kt. 2d.	69. Q. to Kt. 5th, check.
70. K. to R. 2d,	

and draws, as, if Black plays K. to K. 2d, White replies Q. x R., check, and then Queens the Rook's Pawn.

(*o*) The only move.

GAME No. 29.

Played on August 22d, 1876, commencing at 9 A. M.

TIME, 4 HOURS 45 MINUTES.

French Defence.

White (Mr. Davidson).	*Black* (Mr. Elson).
1. P. to K. 4th.	1. P. to K. 3d.
2. P. to Q. 4th.	2. P. to Q. 4th.
3. P. x P.	3. P. x P.
4. Kt. to K. B. 3d.	4. Kt. to K. B. 3d.
5. B. to Q. 3d.	5. B. to Q. 3d.
6. Castles.	6. Castles.
7. B. to K. Kt. 5th.	7. B. to K. Kt. 5th.
8. Q. Kt. to Q. 2d.	8. Q. Kt. to Q. 2d.
9. P. to Q. B. 3d.	9. P. to Q. B. 3d.
10. Q. to B. 2d. (*a*)	10. P. to K. R. 3d.
11. B. to R. 4th.	11. Q. to B. 2d.
12. Q. R. to K. sq.	12. Q. R. to K. sq.
13. B. to K. Kt. 3d.	13. R. x R.
14. Kt. x R.	14. R. to K.
15. B. x B.	15. Q. x B.
16. P. to K. B. 3d.	16. B. to K. 3d.
17. Kt. to Q. Kt. 3d.	17. Kt. to K. B. sq.
18. P. to K. B. 4th.	18. Q. to B. 2d. (*b*)
19. P. to K. R 3d.	19. B. to B. sq.
20. Q. to K. B. 2d.	20. Kt. to K. 5th.
21. B. x Kt.	21. R. x B.

White (Mr. Davidson).	*Black* (Mr. Elson).
22. Kt. to Q. B. 5th.	22. R. to K. sq.
23. P. to B. 5th.	23. P. to K. B. 3d.
24. Kt. to Q. B. 2d.	24. P. to Q. Kt. 3d.
25. Kt. to Q. 3d.	25. B. to Q. R. 3d.
26. R. to K. sq.	26. R. x R., check.
27. Kt. from B. 2d x R.	27. Q. to K. 2d.
28. Kt. to K. B. 4th.	28. Q. to K. 5th.
29. Kt. to R. 5th.	29. Q. to K. sq.
30. Kt. to K. B. 4th.	30. Q. to K. 5th.
31. P. to K. Kt. 4th.	31. Kt. to R. 2d.
32. K. to R. 2d.	32. Kt. to Kt. 4th.
33. P. to K. R. 4th. (*c*)	33. Q. x Kt. at K. 8th.
34. Q. x Q.	34. Kt. to B. 6th, check.
35. K. to R. sq.	35. Kt. x Q.
36. Kt. to K. 6th.	36. Kt. to B. 6th.
37. K. to Kt. 2d.	37. Kt. to Q. 7th.
38. K. to Kt. 3d.	38. Kt. to K. 5th, check.
39. K. to B. 4th.	39. B. to B. sq.
40. Kt. to Q. 8th.	40. B. to Q. 2d.
41. P. to Q. R. 4th.	41. K. to B. sq.
42. P. to Q. R. 5th.	42. K. to K. 2d.
43. Kt. to Q. Kt. 7th.	43. B. to B. sq.
44. P. to R. 6th.	44. Kt. to Q. 3d.
45. Kt. x Kt.	45. K. x Kt.
46. P. to Kt. 5th.	46. K. to K. 2d.
47. P. x P.	47. P. x P.

White resigns.

NOTES BY JACOB ELSON.

(*a*) Up to this point, as is often the case in this opening, both parties have made the same moves.

(*b*) Played in order to be able, should White permit it, to play (after White plays P. to B. 5th) the Kt. to Kt. 5th, and afterwards to Kt. 6th, without encountering the fine reply White had in store had the Q. not been played thus. Let us suppose for a moment White to play, with Black's Q. standing at Q. 3d—

19. P. to B. 5th.	19. Kt. to Kt. 5th.
20. P. to K. Kt. 3d.	20. Kt. to K. 6th.
21. P. x B.!	21. Kt. x Q.
22. P. x P., check.	22. K. to R.
20. P. x R. Queens, and wins.	

(c) Overlooking Black's fatal reply. White's game, however, was a difficult one to save.

GAME No. 30.

Played on August 22d, 1876, commencing at 10.10 A. M.

TIME, 1 HOUR 50 MINUTES.

Center Counter Gambit.

White (MR. BIRD).	*Black* (MR. BARBOUR).
1. P. to K. 4th.	1. P. to K. 4th.
2. Kt. to K. B. 3d.	2. P. to Q. 4th. (*a*)
3. P. x P.	3. P. to K. 5th.
4. Q. to K. 2d.	4. P. to K. B. 4th.
5. P. to Q. 3d.	5. Kt. to K. B. 3d.
6. P. x P.	6. P. x P.
7. Kt. to K. Kt. 5th.	7. Q. x Q. P.
8. P. to K. B. 3d.	8. B. to K. B. 4th.
9. Q. Kt. to Q. 2d.	9. P. to K. 6th.
10. Q. x P., check.	10. K. B. to K. 2d.
11. B. to Q. B. 4th.	11. Q. to Q. B. 4th.
12. Q. x Q.	12. B. x Q.
13. Q. Kt. to K. 4th.	13. Kt. x Kt.
14. P. x Kt.	14. B. to K. Kt. 5th.
15. P. to K. R. 3d.	15. B. to K. R. 4th. (*b*)
16. Kt. to K. 6th.	16. B. to K. B. 2d. (*c*)
17. Kt. x K. Kt. P., check.	17. K. to B. sq.
18. R. to K. B. sq.	18. K. x Kt.
19. R. x B., check.	19. K. to Kt. 3d.
20. R. to K. B. 5th.	20. B. to Q. 5th.
21. P. to Q. B. 3d.	21. B. to B. 3d.

White (Mr. Bird).	*Black* (Mr. Barbour).
22. R. to B. 3d.	22. Kt. to Q. B. 3d.
23. R. to Kt. 3d, check.	23. K. to R. 4th.
24. B. to B. 7th, check.	24. K. to R. 5th.
25. R. mates. (*d*)	

NOTES BY W. H. SAYEN.

(*a*) Utterly unsound in a match game with correct play.

(*b*) This loses at once; however, he had no good move.

(*c*) He had nothing better, the game is already lost.

(*d*) This game is a specimen of Mr. Bird's brilliant play, when a weak defence once gives him an opening into an enemy's game.

GAME No. 31.

Played on August 22d, 1876, commencing at 11.30 A. M.

TIME, 2 HOURS 30 MINUTES.

Ruy Lopez's Knight's Game.

White (Mr. Barbour).	*Black* (Mr. Bird).
1. P. to K. 4th.	1. P. to K. 4th.
2. Kt. to K. B. 3d.	2. Kt. to Q. B. 3d.
3. B. to Q. Kt. 5th.	3. P. to Q. R. 3d.
4. B. to R. 4th.	4. Kt. to K. B. 3d.
5. Castles.	5. Kt. x K. P.
6. R. to K. sq.	6. Kt. to Q. B. 4th.
7. B. x Kt.	7. Q. P. x B.
8. P. to Q. 4th. (*a*)	8. Kt. to K. 3d.
9. Kt. x K. P. (*b*)	9. B. to K. 2d.
10. B. to K. 3d.	10. Castles.
11. P. to Q. B. 3d.	11. P. to K. B. 4th.
12. P. to K. B. 4th.	12. R. to B. 3d.
13. Kt. to Q. 2d.	13. Kt. to K. B. sq.
14. B. to B. 2d.	14. Kt. to Kt. 3d.
15. Kt. x Kt.	15. R. x Kt.
16. Q. to Kt. 3d, check.	16. K. to B. sq. (*c*)
17. Kt. to B. 3d.	17. Q. to Q. 4th.
18. P. to Q. B. 4th.	18. Q. to Q. sq.
19. R. to K. 2d.	19. R. to K. 3d.
20. Kt. to K. 5th. (*d*)	20. B. to B. 3d.
21. R. to Q. sq.	21. P. to Q. Kt. 3d.

White (Mr. Barbour).	*Black* (Mr. Bird).
22. Q. R. to K. sq.	22. B. x Kt.
23. R. x B. (*e*)	23. R. x R.
24. R. x R.	24. Q. to K. B. 3d.
25. Q. to K. 3d.	25. B. to Q. 2d.
26. B. to K. sq.	26. P. to Q. R. 4th.
27. B. to Q. B. 3d.	27. R. to K. sq. (*f*)

And the game was abandoned as drawn.

NOTES BY W. H. SAYEN.

(*a*) Much better than Kt. x P. at once. Black must retreat the Kt.

(*b*) If Black capture the Q. P. with Q., he loses the "exchange," as White plays 10. Q. x Q., followed by 11. Kt. to Kt. 6th, dis. check.

(*c*) Black feared the threatened attack of 17. Kt. to K. B. 3d, followed by 18. Kt. to K. 5th, and the move in the text was the safest course to pursue.

(*d*) White has now obtained a decided superiority of position.

(*e*) Q. P. x B. would, we think, have been decidedly better play. 24. R. to Q. sq. could then have been played, followed by K. R. to Q. 2d, and the passed Pawn at K. 5th would soon have become very troublesome. Mr. Barbour, however, thought that the Rook on the open file would prove more advantageous, and played accordingly.

(*f*) We think White might here have gained a considerable advantage by the following line of play:—

28. P. to Q. 5th.	28. Q. to B. 2d, best.
29. R. x R.	29. B. x R., best.
30. Q. to K. 6th.	30. Q. x Q.
31. P. x Q.	31. P. to K. Kt. 3d, best.
32. B. to K. 5th.	32. K. to K. 2d.
33. B. x Q. B. P.	33. P. to Q. Kt. 4th.
34. Q. B. P. x P.	34. P. x P.
35. B. x R. P.	35. K. x K. P.
36. K. to B. 2d.	

And has the advantage, but Bishops being of opposite colors, Black can perhaps draw, or if—

28. P. to Q. 5th.	28. Q. to B. 2d.
29. R. x R.	29. B. x R.
30. Q. to K. 6th.	30. Q. x Q.
31. P. x Q.	31. P. to K. Kt. 3d.
32. B. to B. 6th.	32. P. to Q. B. 4th.
33. B. to Q. 8th.	

And White ought to win.

GAME No. 32.

Played on August 23d, 1876, commencing at 9 A. M.

TIME, 3 HOURS 30 MINUTES.

Falkbeer–Lederer Counter Gambit.

White (Mr. Elson).	*Black* (Mr. Davidson).
1. P. to K. 4th.	1. P. to K. 4th.
2. P. to K. B. 4th.	2. P. to Q. 4th.
3. K. P. x Q. P.	3. P. to K. 5th.
4. B. to Q. Kt. 5th, ch. (*a*)	4. P. to Q. B. 3d.
5. P. x P.	5. P. x P.
6. B. to Q. B. 4th.	6. Kt. to K. B. 3d.
7. P. to Q. 4th.	7. B. to Q. 3d.
8. Kt. to K. 2d.	8. Q. to R. 4th, check. (*b*)
9. P. to Q. B. 3d.	9. Q. to Kt. Q. 2d.
10. Kt. to Kt. 3d.	10. Kt. to Q. Kt. 3d.
11. B. to K. 2d.	11. Q. Kt. to Q. 4th. (*c*)
12. Castles.	12. Q. to B. 2d.
13. Q. to B. 2d.	13. Kt. x B. P.
14. B. x Kt. (*d*)	14. B. x B.
15. Kt. x K. P.	15. B. x R. P., check.
16. K. to R. sq.	16. Kt. to Q. 4th.
17. Q. to Q. 3d.	17. B. to K. B. 5th.
18. Q. to K. B. 3d.	18. P. to K. R. 4th.
19. Kt. to Q. B. 5th.	19. Q. to K. 2d.
20. Q. to K. B. 2d.	20. Q. to K. Kt. 4th.
21. Kt. to K. 4th.	21. Q. to K. 2d.

White (MR. ELSON).	*Black* (MR. DAVIDSON).
22. B. to Q. B. 4th. (*e*)	22. B. to K. 6th.
23. Q. to K. Kt. 3d.	23. Q. x Kt.
24. B. x Kt.	24. P. x B.
25. R. to K. sq.	25. B. to K. 3d.
26. Q. x B.	26. Q. x Q.

Drawn game.

NOTES BY JACOB ELSON.

(*a*) This is considered the best move.

(*b*) Played in the hope that White would interpose B., when the following variation was likely:—

9. B. to Q. 2d.	9. Q. to K. R. 4th.
10. Castles.	10. P. to K. 6th.

(*c*) Curiously enough, White must now submit to the loss of a Pawn, or do worse.

(*d*) Kt. x K. P. at once, seems better.

(*e*). The best move.

GAME No. 33.

Played on August 23d, 1876, commencing at 9 A.M.

TIME, 2 HOURS 30 MINUTES.

King's Bishop's Gambit.

White (MR. ROBERTS).	*Black* (MR. DAVIDSON).
1. P. to K. 4th.	1. P. to K. 4th.
2. P. to K. B. 4th.	2. P. x P.
3. B. to K. 2d. (*a*)	3. P. to Q. 4th. (*b*)
4. P. x P. (*c*)	4. Q. x P. (*d*)
5. K. Kt. to B. 3d.	5. Q. Kt. to B. 3d.
6. Kt. to B. 3d.	6. Q. to Q. sq.
7. P. to Q. 4th.	7. B. to Q. 3d.
8. Castles	8. Kt. to R. 3d.
9. Kt. to K. 4th.	9. Castles.
10. Kt. to Kt. 5th fr. B. 3d.	10. P. to B. 3d.
11. B. to B. 4th, check.	11. K. to R. sq.
12. Kt. to K. 6th.	12. B. x Kt.
13. B. x B.	13. R. to K. sq.
14. P. to Q. 5th.	14. P. to K. Kt. 4th.
15. Q. to R. 5th. (*e*)	15. B. to B. sq.
16. B. to Q. 2d. (*f*)	16. R. x B.
17. P. x R.	17. Q. to Q. 5th, check.
18. K. to R. sq.	18. Q. x Kt.
19. K. R. to K. sq. (*g*)	19. Q. to Kt. 3d.
20. Q. to B. 3d.	20. Kt. to B. 4th.
21. B. to B. 3d.	21. K. Kt. to Q. 5th.

White (Mr. Roberts).	*Black* (Mr. Davidson).
22. B. x Kt.	22. Kt. x B.
23. Q. x Kt. P.	23. R. to K. sq.
24. Q. to Q. 5th. (*h*)	24. Kt. x B. P.
25. Q. to Q. 7th.	25. Kt. x Q. R.
26. R. x Kt.	26. R. to K. 2d.
27. Q. to Q. 8th.	27. Q. to K. sq.
28. Q. x Q.	28. R. x Q.
29. R. to K. sq.	29. B. to Q. 3d.
30. K. to Kt. sq.	30. B. to K. 4th.
31. R. to Q. sq.	31. R. x P.
32. R. to Q. 8th, check.	32. K. to Kt. 2d.
33. P. to Q. Kt. 3d.	33. R. to Q. 3d.
34. R. x R.	34. B. x R.
35. K. to B. 2d.	35. P. to K. B. 4th.
36. K. to K. 2d.	36. K. to B. 3d.

And Black wins.

NOTES BY W. H. SAYEN.

(*a*) A novelty seldom played, but considered very strong by Jaenisch.

(*b*) Q. to R. 5th, check, followed by 4. P. to Q. 3d, and if 5. P. to Q. 4th—5. Q. to K. B. 3d seems the better defence. The move in the text gives White the better game.

(*c*) P. to K. 5th, followed by 6. P. to Q. 4th, seems to us to be stronger, for should Black attempt to retain the P. by P. to K. Kt. 4th, White soon obtains a decided superiority of position.

(*d*) Here the *Handbuch* gives 4. Q. to R. 5th, check, but gives White a winning game in the variations that ensue.

(*e*) White here chose a decidedly inferior line of play, the correct move was Kt. x B., *i. e.*:—

15. Kt. x B.	15. Q. x Kt., best.
16. Q. to R. 5th.	16. Q. to B. sq.

17. R. to B. 3d.	17. P. to Kt. 5th, best.
18. B. x Kt. P.	18. R. to K. 8th, check.
19. K. to B. 2d.	19. Kt. x B., check.
20. Q. x Kt.	20. Q. to K. sq.
21. Q. x K. B. P.	21. Q. to K. 7th, check.
22. K. to Kt. 3d, and wins.	
Or if—	17. Kt. to K. 4th.
18. R. to R. 3d.	18. Kt. to B. 2d.
19. B. x Kt., and wins.	
Or if—	17. R. x B.
18. P. x R.	18. Q. to Kt. 2d.
19. B. to Q. 2d.	19. Kt. to K. 2d.
20. B. to B. 3d.	20. Kt. to Kt. sq. fr. R. 3d.
21. R. to Q. sq., and wins.	

(*f*) 16. R. to Q. sq. was obviously not good on account of Kt. to Q. 4th, and if 17. R. x Kt., then 17. R. x B. We think 16. P. to Q. B. 3d, followed by P. to Q. Kt. 3d, and B. to Kt. 2d, would have been much stronger. The move in the text was certainly not made with due consideration.

(*g*) Here White might have played B. to B. 3d, *i. e.* :—

19. B. to B. 3d.	19. Q. x K. P.
20. Q. x Kt. P.	20. B. to Kt. 2d.
21. Q. x B. P., and wins at least a Pawn.	
Or if—	19. B. to Kt. 2d.
20. B. x B. P.	20. Q. to Kt. 3d.
21. Q. x Q.	21. P. x Q.
22. B. x Kt. P., with the best game.	

(*h*) The game probably cannot be saved, but R. to Q. sq. offered the best chance.

GAME No. 34.

Played on August 23d, 1876, commencing at 9 A. M.

TIME, 4 HOURS.

French Defence.

White (MR. MASON).	*Black* (MR. ELSON).
1. P. to K. 4th.	1. P. to K. 3d.
2. P. to Q. 4th.	2. P. to Q. 4th.
3. Kt. to Q. B. 3d.	3. B. to Kt. 5th. (*a*)
4. P. x P.	4. P. x P.
5. Kt. to B. 3d.	5. K. Kt. to B. 3d.
6. B. to Q. 3d.	6. Castles.
7. Castles.	7. B. to Q. 3d.
8. Kt. to K. 2d.	8. B. to K. Kt. 5th.
9. Kt. to Kt. 3d.	9. Kt. to Q. 2d.
10. B. to K. 3d.	10. P. to Q. B. 3d.
11. P. to Q. B. 3d.	11. Q. to B. 2d.
12. P. to K. R. 3d.	12. B. to K. 3d.
13. Q. to Q. 2d.	13. Q. R. to K. sq. (*b*)
14. Q. R. to K. sq.	14. K. to R. sq. (*c*)
15. B. to Q. Kt. sq.	15. P. to Q. R. 3d.
16. B. to K. Kt. 5th.	16. B. x Kt.
17. P. x B.	17. Kt. to Kt. sq.
18. P. to K. Kt. 4th.	18. P. to K. B. 3d.
19. B. to K. B. 4th.	19. Q. to Q. sq.
20. B. to Q. 6th.	20. R. to B. 2d.
21. P. to Kt. 5th.	21. Kt. to B. sq.

White (Mr. Mason).	*Black* (Mr. Elson).
22. B. x Kt.	22. K. R. x B.
23. Q. to B. 2d.	23. P. to K. Kt. 3d.
24. Kt. to R. 4th.	24. P. to K. B. 4th. (*d*)
25. Q. to Q. 2d. (*e*)	25. B. to Q. B. sq.
26. Q. to K. B. 4th.	26. R. to K. 2d.
27. Kt. to K. B. 3d.	27. K. R. to K. sq.
28. Kt. to K. 5th.	28. K. to Kt. 2d.
29. P. to K. R. 4th.	29. R. to K. 3d.
30. P. to K. Kt. 4th.	30. R. fr. K. 3d to K. 2d.
31. P. x P.	31. B. x P.
32. B. x B.	32. R. to B. sq.
33. Q. to Kt. 4th.	33. P. x B.
34. R. x P.	34. R. x R.
35. Q. x R.	35. Q. to K. B. sq.
36. Q. to K. Kt. 4th.	36. K. to R. sq.
37. R. to K. B. sq.	37. Q. to Kt. 2d.
38. P. to R. 5th.	38. R. to Q. B. 2d.
39. P. to R. 6th.	Resigns.

NOTES BY JACOB ELSON.

(*a*) Kt. to K. B. 3d is now considered a better reply.

(*b*) By playing 13. B. x Kt., and afterwards Q. x Kt. P., Black would have obviously lost the Q. The correct move, however, instead of the move made was to play—

	13. B. x Kt.
14. P. x B.	14. Kt. to K. 5th.
15. B. x Kt., best.	15. P. x B.
16. Kt. to Kt. 5th.	16. B. to Q. 4th.
17. B. to K. B. 4th.	17. Q. to Q. sq.
18. P. to Q. B. 4th.	

The best move, as Black threatened to win Kt. by P. to K. R.

3d; the other two moves at White's command, viz., P. to K. R. 4th, or B. to Q. 6th, being decidedly inferior.

	18. B. x Q. B. P.
19. Kt. x K. P.	19. B. to Q. 4th, with the preferable game.

(*c*) This and the next move of Black are purposeless and useless. They are intended as waiting moves, Black hoping that White might get up some premature attack. They only result, however, in hampering Black's game.

(*d*) Missing the opportunity of equalizing the game by B. to B. 2d, the move made, though seemingly strongly defensive, hampers Black's game beyond any hope of recovery.

(*e*) White plays the remainder of the game with his usual judgment and ability.

GAME No. 35.

Played on August 23d, 1876, commencing at 9.50 A.M.

TIME, 7 HOURS.

Scotch Gambit.

White (MR. JUDD).	*Black* (MR. BIRD).
1. P. to K. 4th.	1. P. to K. 4th.
2. Kt. to K. B. 3d.	2. Kt. to Q. B. 3d.
3. P. to Q. 4th.	3. P. x P.
4. Kt. x P.	4. B. to Q. B. 4th. (*a*)
5. B. to K. 3d.	5. Q. to K. B. 3d, best.
6. P. to Q. B. 3d.	6. Q. to K. Kt. 3d. (*b*)
7. Kt. to Q. 2d.	7. Kt. x Kt.
8. P. x Kt.	8. B. to Q. Kt. 5th.
9. P. to K. B. 3d. (*c*)	9. Kt. to K. 2d.
10. Q. to Q. B. 2d.	10. P. to Q. B. 3d.
11. P. to K. Kt. 3d. (*d*)	11. P. to Q. 4th.
12. B. to Q. 3d.	12. P. x P.
13. P. x P. (*e*)	13. B. to K. Kt. 5th.
14. Castles.	14. B. x Kt.
15. B. x B.	15. Q. to Q. 3d. (*f*)
16. B. to Q. B. 3d.	16. P. to K. R. 4th.
17. Q. to K. B. 2d.	17. P. to K. B. 4th. (*g*)
18. P. x P.	18. B. to K. R. 6th.
19. K. R. to K.	19. Castles, Q. R.
20. R. to K. 6th.	20. Q. to Q. B. 2d.
21. Q. R. to K. sq.	21. Kt. to Q. 4th.

White (Mr. Judd).	*Black* (Mr. Bird).
22. Q. B. to Q. 2d.	22. Q. to K. B. 2d.
23. B. to K. Kt. 5th.	23. Q. R. to K. sq.
24. Q. to K. 2d. (*h*)	24. Kt. to Q. B. 2d. (*i*)
25. R. to K. 5th. (*j*)	25. R. x R.
26. P. x R.	26. B. x P.
27. Q. to K. B. 2d.	27. B. to K. Kt. 3d!
28. B. x B.	28. Q. x B.
29. B. to K. B. 4th.	29. R. to K. B. sq. (*k*)
30. K. to R. sq.	30. P. to Q. Kt. 3d.
31. Q. to K. B. 3d.	31. K. to Kt. 2d.
32. R. to Q. sq.	32. Kt. to Q. 4th.
33. P. to K. R. 4th.	33. Q. to K. 3d.
34. K. to Kt. 2d.	34. R. to K. B. 4th. (*l*)
35. P. to Q. R. 3d.	35. P. to Q. R. 4th.
36. R. to Q. B. sq.	36. P. to K. Kt. 4th. (*m*)
37. P. x P.	37. P. to K. R. 5th.
38. R. to K. B. sq. (*n*)	38. Q. to K. B. 2d. (*o*)
39. Q. to K. 4th.	39. P. x Kt. P.
40. P. to K. 6th. (*p*)	40. Q. to K. R. 2d.
41. P. to K. 7th. (*q*)	41. Q. to R. 7th, check.
42. K. to B. 3d.	42. P. to K. Kt. 7th.

And Mr. Judd resigns, as the game is forced.

NOTES BY W. H. SAYEN.

(*a*) Von Bilgner and Der Laza consider this move good, but not so good as Q. to R. 5th, which, with the best play, they consider wins.

(*b*) K. Kt. to K. 2d is given by the authorities as the best move. The one in the text, however, seems good, being both attacking and threatening.

(*c*) Seemingly the best move, as Q. to B. 2d could not evidently be played on account of threatened P. to Q. 4th on Black's next move.

(*d*) In order to free the action of the K. B., which important piece is completely paralyzed by the position of the Black Queen.

(*e*) Had he retaken with K. B., the isolated Queen's Pawn must ultimately fall a sacrifice to Black's attacks.

(*f*) An excellent move; in fact Black's last few moves have been very fine, and, with apparently the best play on the part of White, he has steadily improved his position. He now attacks the Q. P., threatening also to Castle Q. R., and commence a formidable attack with the King's Pawns.

(*g*) This is Mr. Bird all over. It is yet doubtful, after a most careful analysis, whether this move was sound, though Mr. Bird contends that it is. The analysis is too extended for publication here, and the reader can best judge from the remainder of the game whether White could have held his advantage.

(*h*) This undoubtedly weak move cost White serious embarrassment, and eventually lost the Pawn. 24. R. x R. was a better move, *i. e.*—

24. R. x R., check.	24. R. x R.
25. R. x R., check.	25. Q. x R.
26. P. to Q. R. 3d.	26. Q. to K. B. 2d.

And White retains the Pawn and ought to win by B. to K. B. sq., followed by P. to K. B. 6th.

(*i*) This virtually wins the Pawns.

(*j*) R. to K. 7th, though promising, would not have resulted more favorably, *i. e.* :—

25. R. to K. 7th.	25. Q. x Q. R. P.
26. B. to Q. B. 4th.	26. Q. to Q. R. 4th.
27. B. to K. B. 4th.	27. R. x R.
28. Q. x R.	28. B. x P.

And Black has the best of it.

(*k*) Selected with great judgment. The threatening position of this Rook paralyzes White's game for many moves, and also prevents the capture of the Q. R. P. besides threatening Kt. to Q. 4th.

(*l*) Patiently getting his pieces into position, anticipating the removal of the Rook from Q. sq., when he can safely commence the onslaught on the K. side.

(*m*) This fine move is worthy of Mr. Bird, and is perfectly sound with the best analyses.

(*n*) With everything considered, R. to K. R. sq. would have been the best line of defence, *i. e.*—

38. R. to K. R. sq.	38. P. x P.
39. R. to R. 7th, check.	39. K. to R. 3d. (1)
40. Q. to Q. 3d, check.	40. P. to Kt. 3d.
41. B. x Kt. P.,	

with the best game, as he threatens Q. to Q. 4th.

(1)

	39. K. to B. sq.
40. R. to R. 8th, check, and can draw.	

(*o*) Again finely played, opening the K. R. 2d square, and winning the game.

(*p*) He has nothing better, as the game is irretrievable.

(*q*) If—

41. R. to K. R. sq.	41. Kt. x B., check.
42. K. x P.	42. R. x P., check.
43. K. x Kt.	43. R. to Kt. 4th, check, and wins.

GAME No. 36.

Played on August 23d, 1876, commencing at 9 A.M.

TIME, 4 HOURS.

Irregular Opening.

White (Mr. Ware).	*Black* (Mr. Barbour).
1. P. to Q. 4th.	1. P. to Q. 4th.
2. P. to K. B. 4th.	2. Kt. to K. B. 3d.
3. Kt. to K. B. 3d.	3. Kt. to K. 5th. (*a*)
4. P. to K. 3d.	4. P. to K. Kt. 3d.
5. B. to Q. 3d.	5. B. to Kt. 2d.
6. Castles.	6. P. to K. B. 4th.
7. B. to Q. 2d.	7. Kt. to Q. 2d. (*b*)
8. B. to K. sq.	8. P. to Q. B. 4th.
9. P. to Q. B. 3d.	9. P. to B. 5th.
10. B. x Kt.	10. Q. P. x B.
11. Kt. to Kt. 5th.	11. Kt. to Q. Kt. 3d.
12. Kt. to Q. 2d.	12. P. to K. R. 3d.
13. Kt. to R. 3d.	13. B. to K. 3d.
14. R. to B. 2d.	14. P. to Q. R. 3d.
15. Kt. to K. B. sq.	15. Kt. to Q. 4th.
16. P. to Q. Kt. 4th.	16. P. to Q. Kt. 3d.
17. P. to Q. R. 4th.	17. Kt. to K. B. 3d.
18. R. to Q. Kt. sq.	18. B. to Q. 4th. (*c*)
19. K. R. to Q. R. 2d.	19. Castles.
20. Kt. to B. 2d.	20. P. to K. 3d.
21. P. to K. R. 3d.	21. K. to R. 2d.

White (Mr. Ware).	*Black* (Mr. Barbour).
22. Kt. to R. 2d.	22. R. to Q. R. 2d.
23. Kt. to R. sq.	23. P. to K. Kt. 4th.
24. P. to K. Kt. 3d.	24. P. x P.
25. Kt. P. x P.	25. R. to Kt. sq.
26. R. to K. Kt. 2d.	26. B. to K. R. sq.
27. Q. R. to Kt. 2d.	27. R. x R., check.
28. R. x R.	28. P. to Q. R. 4th.
29. P. to Kt. 5th.	29. Q. to K. sq.
30. Kt. to Kt. 3d.	30. B. to K. Kt. 2d.
31. Kt. fr. R. 2d to B. sq.	31. B. to K. R. sq.
32. Q. to K. 2d.	32. R. to Q. B. 2d.
33. K. to R. 2d.	33. B. to Q. Kt. 2d.
34. Kt. to Q. 2d.	34. B. to Q. 4th.
35. Kt. fr. Q. 2d to B. sq.	35. B. to K. Kt. 2d.
36. Q. to R. 2d.	36. B. to K. B. sq.
37. Q. to Q. B. 2d.	37. B. to Q. 3d.
38. Kt. to Q. 2d.	38. R. to K. Kt. 2d.
39. Kt. fr. Q. 2d to B. sq.	39. R. to Kt. 3d.
40. Q. to K. 2d.	40. B. to B. sq.
41. K. to R. sq.	41. R. to Kt. sq.
42. K. to R. 2d.	42. Q. to K. B. 2d.
43. Kt. to Q. 2d.	43. Q. to Q. B. 2d.
44. Kt. to R. 5th.	44. R. x R., check. (*d*)
45. K. x R.	45. Kt. to K. sq.
46. B. to R. 4th.	46. Q. to K. B. 2d.
47. B. to Q. 8th.	47. Q. to Kt. 2d.
48. Kt. to B. 6th, check.	48. Kt. x Kt.
49. B. x Kt.	49. B. to Kt. 2d.
50. B. x B.	50. Q. x B., check.
51. K. to R. 2d.	51. Q. to Q. B. 2d.
52. P. to K. R. 4th.	52. Q. to K. Kt. 2d

White (Mr. Ware).	*Black* (Mr. Barbour).
53. P. to R. 5th.	53. K. to R. sq.
54. Kt. to Q. Kt. sq.	54. Q. to K. Kt. sq.
55. Kt. to Q. 2d.	55. K. to R. 2d.

And the game was abandoned as drawn. (*e*)

NOTES BY W. H. SAYEN.

(*a*) We would prefer P. to K. 3d, followed by 4. P. to Q. Kt. 3d, and 5. B. to Q. Kt. 2d.

(*b*) P. to Q. B. 4th might here have been safely played, and we think would have improved his game, *i. e.*:—

	7. P. to Q. B. 4th.
8. B. to Kt. 5th, check.	8. K. to B. sq.!
9. P. to Q. B. 3d.	9. P. to Q. B. 5th.
10. B. to R. 4th!	10. P. to Q. R. 3d.
11. B. to B. 2d.	11. P. to Q. Kt. 4th.

With the freer game.

(*c*) The game already looks *drawish*. It presents something of the appearance of the Macedonian Phalanx, impenetrable.

(*d*) The quickest method of producing the inevitable draw.

(*e*) If—

Kt. x B. P.	B. x Kt.
Q. x B.	Q. to K. Kt. 5th, etc.

GAME No. 37.

Played on August 23d, 1876, commencing at 1 P. M.

TIME, 4 HOURS.

Centre Counter Gambit.

White (Mr. Barbour).	*Black* (Mr. Ware).
1. P. to K. 4th.	1. P. to Q. 4th.
2. P. x P.	2. Q. x P.
3. Kt. to Q. B. 3d.	3. Q. to Q. sq. (*a*)
4. B. to K. 2d.	4. P. to Q. B. 3d.
5. P. to K. R. 3d.	5. B. to K. B. 4th.
6. Kt. to K. B. 3d.	6. P. to K. 3d.
7. P. to Q. R. 3d.	7. P. to K. R. 3d.
8. P. to Q. 4th.	8. Kt. to B. 3d.
9. Castles.	9. B. to K. 2d.
10. B. to K. 3d.	10. Q. Kt. to Q. 2d.
11. Kt. to K. R. 4th.	11. B. to R. 2d.
12. P. to B. 4th.	12. Kt. to Kt. 3d.
13. Kt. to B. 3d.	13. Q. Kt. to Q. 4th.
14. B. to B. sq. (*b*)	14. Q. to B. 2d.
15. Kt. x Kt.	15. Kt. x Kt.
16. Kt. to K. 5th.	16. Castles, K. R.
17. P. to Q. B. 4th.	17. Kt. to K. B. 3d.
18. B. to Q. 3d.	18. Q. R. to Q. sq.
19. P. to Q. Kt. 4th.	19. P. to Q. R. 4th.
20. P. to Q. B. 5th.	20. P. x Kt. P.
21. P. x P.	21. t. to Q. 4th. (*c*)

White (Mr. Barbour).	*Black* (Mr. Ware).
22. B. x B, check.	22. K. x B.
23. B. to Q. 2d.	23. K. to Kt. sq.
24. Q. to Q. Kt. 3d.	24. B. to B. 3d.
25. Q. R. to Q. sq.	25. Kt. to K. 2d.
26. B. to K. sq.	26. R. to Q. 4th.
27. R. to Q. 3d.	27. K. R. to Q. sq.
28. B. to B. 2d.	28. B. x Kt.
29. B. P. x B.	29. Kt. to Kt. 3d.
30. R. to K. sq.	30. Q. to Q. 2d.
31. R. to K. B. 3d.	31. Q. to K. 2d.
32. R. to K. B. sq.	32. K. R. to Q. 2d.
33. P. to K. Kt. 3d.	33. Q. to Kt. 4th.
34. B. to K. 3d.	34. Q. to R. 4th.
35. B. to B. 2d. (*d*)	35. Q. x R. P.
36. R. to Q. R. sq.	36. K. to R. 2d. (*e*)
37. P. to Q. Kt. 5th.	37. Q. to K. Kt. 5th. (*f*)
38. P. x P.	38. P. x P.
39. R. to Q. R. 8th.	39. Kt. x K. P. (*g*)
40. Q. P. x Kt.	40. R. to Q. 8th, check.
41. K. to Kt. 2d.	41. Q. to R. 4th.
42. Q. to B. 2d, check.	42. K. R. to Q. 6th. (*h*)
43. Q. x R., check.	43. R. x Q.
44. R. x R.	44. Q. x K. P.
45. R. to Q. 8th fr. R. 8th.	45. P. to K. B. 3d.
46. R. to K. 3d. (*i*)	46. Q. to K. B. 4th.
47. R. to Q. 6th.	47. Q. x P.
48. R. fr. K. 3d x P.	48. Q. to Q. Kt. 4th.
49. R. x Q. B. P.	49. Q. to Q. 4th, check.
50. K. to Kt. sq.	50. Q. to Q. 8th, check.
51. R. to K. sq.	51. Q. to Q. 4th.
52. R. to B. 7th.	52. Q. to Q. 3d.
53. R. fr. K. sq. to K. 7th.	53. Q. to Q. 8th, check.

White (Mr. Barbour).	*Black* (Mr. Ware).
54. B. to K. sq.	54. K. to R. sq.
55. R. fr. B. 7th to Q. 7th.	55. Q. to B. 8th.
56. K. to Kt. 2d.	56. Q. to B. 3d, check.
57. K. to Kt. sq.	57. Q. to B. 8th.
58. K. to B. 2d. (*j*)	58. Q. to B. 7th, check.
59. K. to K. 3d.	59. Q. to B. 8th, check.
60. K. to Q. 4th.	60. Q. to Kt. 7th, check.
61. K. to B. 5th.	61. Q. to B. 7th, check.
62. K. to Kt. 6th.	62. Q. to B. 8th.
63. R. to Q. B. 7th.	63. Q. to Q. 8th.
64. K. to Kt. 7th.	64. Q. to Q. 4th, check.
65. K. to B. 8th.	65. Q. to B. 4th, check.
66. K. to Kt. 7th.	66. Q. to Q. 4th, check.
67. K. to R. 7th.	67. Q. to R. 7th, check.
68. K. to Kt. 8th.	68. Q. to Kt. 6th, check.
69. R. to Kt. 7th.	69. Q. to Q. 4th.
70. R. x P.	70. Q. to K. 4th, check.
71. R. fr. K. Kt. 7th to B. 7th.	71. K. to Kt. sq.
72. B. to B. 3d.	72. Q. x Kt. P.
73. K. to R. 8th.	73. Q. x R. (*k*)
74. R. x Q.	74. P. to B. 4th.
75. B. to K. 5th.	

And White finally inadvertently stalemated his adversary. (*l*)

NOTES BY W. H. SAYEN.

(*a*) Best. Some authorities prefer, however, Q. to Q. R. 4th.

(*b*) Better than taking the Kt. at once.

(*c*) It is evident he cannot capture the Q. P. with R.

(*d*) The R. P. was offered, in order to take the Q. out of play and obtain an attack on the Q. side.

(*c*) To avoid the check from the R., after the contemplated sacrifice of the Kt.

(*f*) Q. to R. 4th looks much stronger, *i. e.*:—

	37. Q. to R. 4th.
38. P. x P.	38. P. x P.
39. R. to R. 8th.	39. Kt. x K. P.

And wins.

(*g*) Unsound, but requiring the nicest play to overcome it.

(*h*) We would have preferred to try the effect of 42. P. to K. B. 4th, and if P. x P. en pass. ch., play P. to Kt. 3d. If he play P. to Kt. 3d at once, then—

	42. P. to K. Kt. 3d.
43. Q. x R.	43. R. x Q.
44. R. x B. P., mate.	

(*i*) The play of the Rooks by Mr. Barbour is very fine.

(*j*) The commencement of a fine combination which will repay study.

(*k*) Compulsory, to escape the threatened mate.

(*l*) A singular fatality seems to have followed Mr. Barbour in this Tournament.

GAME No. 38.

Played on August 24th, 1876, commencing at 2 P. M.

TIME, 2 HOURS.

Ruy Lopez's Knight's Game.

White (Mr. Davidson).	*Black* (Mr. Roberts).
1. P. to K. 4th.	1. P. to K. 4th.
2. Kt. to K. B. 3d.	2. Kt. to Q. B. 3d.
3. B. to Kt. 5th.	3. K. Kt. to K. 2d. (*a*)
4. Castles. (*b*)	4. P. to K. Kt. 3d.
5. P. to Q. B. 3d. (*c*)	5. B. to K. Kt. 2d.
6. P. to Q. 4th.	6. P. x P.
7. Kt. x P. (*d*)	7. Kt. x Kt. (*e*)
8. P. x Kt.	8. P. to Q. B. 3d.
9. B. to R. 4th.	9. Q. to Kt. 3d. (*f*)
10. B. to K. 3d. (*g*)	10. Q. x Kt. P.
11. Kt. to Q. 2d.	11. Q. to Kt. 3d. (*h*)
12. Kt. to B. 4th.	12. Q. to B. 2d.
13. Q. to Q. 2d.	13. Castles. (*i*)
14. B. to B. 4th.	14. Q. to Q. sq.
15. Kt. to Q. 6th.	15. Q. to Kt. 3d. (*j*)
16. K. R. to Q. sq.	16. P. to Q. R. 4th.
17. Q. R. to Kt. sq.	17. Q. to R. 3d.
18. B. to K. Kt. 5th.	18. P. to K. B. 3d.
19. B. to Q. Kt. 3d, check.	19. K. to R. sq.
20. Kt. to B. 7th, check.	20. K. to Kt. sq. (*k*)

White (Mr. Davidson).	*Black* (Mr. Roberts).
21. Kt. to Q. 6th, check.	21. K. to R. sq.
22. Q. to B. 4th.	22. P. to Q. R. 5th.
23. Kt. to B. 7th, check.	23. K. to Kt. sq.
24. Kt. to R. 6th, double ch.	24. K. to R. sq.

And, both parties persisting in the same moves, the game was abandoned as drawn. (*l*)

NOTES BY W. H. SAYEN.

(*a*) First played in 1497, we believe. Anderson also played it against Newman in 1865, and Paulsen against Boden in the same year.

(*b*) Not so strong as 4. P. to Q. 4th first, *i. e.*—

4. P. to Q. 4th.	4. P. x P.
5. Castles.	5. P. to Q. 4th.
6. R. to K. sq.	6. B. to Kt. 5th.
7. B. x Q. Kt., check.	7. P. x B.
8. Q. x Q. P.	8. B. x K. Kt.
9. P. x B.	9. Q. to Q. 3d.
10. K. P. x P.	10. B. P. x P.
11. Kt. to Q. B. 3d.	11. P. to Q. B. 3d.
12. B. to B. 4th.	12. Q. to Kt. 3d, check.
13. K. to R. sq.,	

with a fine game.

(*c*) Again we prefer P. to Q. 4th.

(*d*) Mr. Boden here played against Paulsen 7. P. x P., and the reply was 7. P. to Q. 4th, *i. e.* :—

7. P. x P.	7. P. to Q. 4th.
8. P. x P.	8. Kt. x P.
9. R. to K. sq., check.	9. B. to K. 3d.
10. B. x Kt., check.	

This was a bad move. He should have played B. to K. Kt. 5th, and had the better game.

(*e*) We prefer castles first, followed by 8. P. to Q. R. 3d.

(*f*) Weak. 9. P. to Q. 4th much stronger, *i. e.*:—

	9. P. to Q. 4th.
10. P. to K. 5th.	10. Q. to Kt. 3d.
11. B. to Kt. 3d.	11. Kt. to B. 4th.
12. B. to K. 3d.	12. Kt. x B.
13. P. x Kt.	13. B. to K. 3d.
14. K. to R. sq.	14. Q. R. to Q. sq.

And we much prefer Black's game.

(*g*) We doubt if this was sound. It does not even yield a compensating attack, but the defence did not make the best answering moves.

(*h*) 11. P. to Q. 4th seems to us to have been the move. The move in the text appeared to be good, but subjected him to a severe attack, *i. e.*:—

	11. P. to Q. 4th.
12. P. to K. 5th.	12. Kt. to B. 4th.
13. B. to Kt. 3d.	13. B. to K. 3d.
14. R. to Kt. sq.	14. Q. to B. 6th.
15. R. to B. sq.	15. Q. to Kt. 4th.
16. Kt. to B. 3d.	16. Kt. x B.
17. P. x Kt.,	17. Q. to K. 2d.

and remains with the Pawn.

(*i*) Again 13. P. to Q. 4th was much better, *i. e.*:—

	13. P. to Q. 4th.
14. B. to B. 4th.	14. Q. to Q. sq.
15. Kt. to Q. 6th, check.	15. K. to B. sq.
16. Q. to Q. Kt. 4th.	16. P. to Q. Kt. 4th.
17. B. to Kt. 3d.	17. P. to Q. R. 4th.
18. Q. to B. 5th.	18. P. to Q. R. 5th.
19. B. to B. 2d,	19. B. to K. 3d.

and retains his pawn, though his position is somewhat uncomfortable.

(*j*) Better here 15. P. to Q. R. 4th.

(*k*) It is evident he loses if he take the Kt., *i. e.*:—

	19. R. x Kt.
20. B. x R.	20. P. x Q. B.
21. Q. x Kt. P.	21. Kt. to K. Kt. sq.
22. Q. to Q. 8th, and wins.	

(*l*) White is utterly powerless to do more than draw.

GAME No. 39.

Played on August 24th, 1876, commencing at 9 A.M.

TIME, 5 HOURS 30 MINUTES.

Ruy Lopez's Knight's Game.

White (MR. BIRD).	*Black* (MR. JUDD).
1. P. to K. 4th.	1. P. to K. 4th.
2. Kt. to K. B. 3d.	2. Kt. to Q. B. 3d.
3. B. to Kt. 5th.	3. P. to Q. R. 3d.
4. B. to R. 4th.	4. Kt. to K. B. 3d.
5. Q. to K. 2d. (*a*)	5. B. to K. B. 4th.
6. P. to Q. B. 3d.	6. P. to Q. Kt. 4th.
7. B. to Kt. 3d.	7. P. to Q. 3d. (*b*)
8. P. to Q. R. 4th.	8. R. to Q. Kt. sq.
9. P. x P.	9. P. x P.
10. P. to Q. 3d.	10. Kt. to K. 2d.
11. B. to K. 3d.	11. Kt. to Kt. 3d.
12. P. to K. Kt. 3d.	12. B. to Kt. 3d.
13. Q. Kt. to Q. 2d.	13. P. to Q. B. 3d.
14. Kt. to B. sq.	14. Castles.
15. B. x B.	15. Q. x B.
16. Kt. to K. 3d. (*c*)	16. B. to K. 3d.
17. B. x B.	17. P. x B.
18. P. to K. R. 4th.	18. Kt. to R. sq.
19. Castles, K. R.	19. P. to K. R. 3d.
20. P. to Q. Kt. 4th.	20. Q. R. to R. sq.
21. K. to Kt. 2d.	21. Kt. to Kt. 3d.

White (Mr. Bird).	*Black* (Mr. Judd).
22. Kt. to R. 2d.	22. R. to R. 2d.
23. P. to R. 5th.	23. Kt. to R. sq.
24. R. x R.	24. Q. x R. (*d*)
25. Kt. fr. R. 2d to Kt. 4th.	25. Q. to R. 6th.
26. Kt. x Kt., check.	26. R. x Kt.
27. Q. to Q. 2d.	27. R. to B. sq.
28. P. to Q. B. 4th.	28. R. to Kt. sq.
29. R. to Q. B. sq.	29. Kt. to B. 2d.
30. P. x P.	30. P. x P.
31. R. to B. 3d.	31. Q. to R. 2d.
32. Q. to B. sq.	32. R. to Kt. 2d.
33. R. to B. 8th, check.	33. K. to R. 2d.
34. Q. to B. 6th.	34. R. to K. 2d. (*e*)
35. Q. x P.	35. Q. to R. 7th.
36. R. to B. 2d.	36. Q. to Kt. 8th.
37. Q. to B. 4th. (*f*)	37. Kt. to Kt. 4th.
38. R. to B. sq.	38. Q. to Kt. 7th.
39. Q. to B. 3d. (*g*)	39. Q. to K. 7th.
40. R. to K. R. sq. (*h*)	40. R. to K. B. 2d.
41. Kt. to Q. sq.	41. R. to B. 6th. (*i*)
42. Q. to B. sq.	42. R. x P., check.
43. K. x R.	43. Q. to B. 6th, check. (*j*)

And Mr. Bird resigned the game.

NOTES BY W. H. SAYEN.

(*a*) In England this attack is almost exclusively played, and indeed it may well be called one of the strongest.

(*b*) The *Handbuch* here gives castling as the best move, followed by

8. P. to Q. 3d.	8. P. to Q. 3d.
9. B. to K. Kt. 5th.	9. B. to K. 3d.
10. Q. Kt. to Q. 2d.	10. P. to K. R. 3d.

Even game.

(*c*) Mr. Bird planted this Knight very skilfully in a strong position by a neat line of play. It can now be used offensively or defensively as the exigency may require.

(*d*) We now much prefer White's game.

(*e*) He was compelled to surrender the Kt. P. to escape the fatal effects of Q. to K. 8th.

(*f*) This move was most unfortunate, and is only one of the many instances in which a game is lost by ill-considered play. White had here a winning game, *i. e.* :—

37. Q. to Q. Kt. 8th.	37. Q. to Q. Kt. 6th or R. 8th.
38. Q. to K. B. 8th.	38. Q. to R. 2d.
39. R. to Q. B. 8th, and wins.	

Or—

37. Q. to Q. Kt. 8th.	37. P. to K. Kt. 3d.
38. Q. to K. B. 8th.	38. Anything.
39. R. to B. 8th, and wins.	

(*g*) At once losing the advantage. He still had a winning game by R. to B. 2d, followed by Q. to B. 8th, and K. 8th, etc.

(*h*) This move loses the game offhand. He should have given up the R. P., playing Q. to B. 2d, and still hoping for results from the passed Pawn at Q. Kt. 4th.

(*i*) The correct move, and very pretty, finishing the game in style.

(*j*) The mate is forced in three moves, *i. e.* :—

43. Q. to B. 6th, check.	43. K. to R. 2d, or anywhere.
44. Q. to R. 6th, check.	44. K. to Kt. sq.
45. Kt. to B. 6th, mate.	

GAME No. 40.

Played on August 24th, 1876, commencing at 9 A. M.

TIME, 4 HOURS.

Hollandish Opening.

White (Mr. Ware).	*Black* (Mr. Roberts).
1. P. to Q. 4th.	1. P. to K. B. 4th. (*a*)
2. P. to K. B. 4th.	2. P. to K. 3d.
3. Kt. to K. B. 3d.	3. Kt. to K. B. 3d.
4. P. to K. 3d.	4. B. to K. 2d.
5. B. to Q. 3d.	5. Castles.
6. Castles.	6. P. to Q. Kt. 3d.
7. P. to Q. R. 3d.	7. B. to Kt. 2d.
8. B. to Q. 2d.	8. Q. to K. sq.
9. B. to K. 2d.	9. K. to R. sq.
10. Kt. to K. 5th.	10. P. to Q. 3d.
11. B. to K. B. 3d.	11. Kt. to K. 5th. (*b*)
12. Kt. to Q. 3d.	12. Kt. to Q. 2d.
13. Kt. to B. 2d.	13. Q. Kt. to B. 3d.
14. Kt. to Q. B. 3d.	14. Q. to Kt. 3d.
15. Q. Kt. x Kt.	15. Kt. x Kt. (*c*)
16. Kt. x Kt.	16. B. x Kt.
17. B. x B.	17. P. x B. (*d*)
18. B. to K. sq.	18. P. to Q. 4th.
19. R. to Q. B. sq.	19. P. to Q. B. 4th.
20. P. to Q. B. 3d.	20. Q. R. to Q. B. sq.
21. R. to Q. B. 2d.	21. R. to Q. B. 2d.

White (Mr. Ware).	*Black* (Mr. Roberts).
22. Q. R. to K. B. 2d.	22. B. to Q. 3d.
23. R. to Q. 2d.	23. P. to K. R. 3d.
24. P. to K. Kt. 4th.	24. P. x P.
25. B. P. x P.	25. K. R. to Q. B. sq.
26. B. to Kt. 3d.	26. Q. to B. 3d.
27. Q. to K. 2d.	27. K. to R. 2d.
28. P. to K. R. 4th.	28. Q. to B. 2d.
29. K. to Kt. 2d.	29. P. to K. Kt. 3d.
30. K. to R. 3d.	30. R. to B. 3d.
31. Q. to R. 2d.	31. P. to K. R. 4th.
32. Q. to K. 2d.	32. P. x P., check.
33. Q. x P.	33. Q. to B. 4th.
34. R. to K. Kt. sq.	34. K. to R. 3d.
35. Q. R. to Kt. 2d.	35. Q. x Q.
36. K. x Q.	36. R. to B. 8th.
37. R. x R.	37. R. x R.
38. R. to R. 2d.	38. P. to Q. R. 4th.
39. P. to R. 5th.	39. P. x P.
40. R. x P., check.	40. K. to Kt. 3d.
41. R. to R. 2d. (*e*)	41. B. to K. 2d.
42. R. to K. 2d.	42. P. to Kt. 4th.
43. R. to K. B. 2d.	43. B. to Q. 3d. (*f*)
44. B. to R. 4th.	44. P. to Kt. 5th.
45. P. x P.	45. P. x P.
46. R. to Q. 2d.	46. P. to Kt. 6th.
47. B. to K. sq.	47. R. to B. 7th.
48. R. x R.	48. P. x R.
49. B. to B. 2d.	49. B. to Kt. 5th.
50. B. to B. sq.	

And the game was abandoned as drawn. (*g*)

NOTES BY W. H. SAYEN.

(*a*) Stein in Variations for Amateurs, 1775, first mentions this move.

(*b*) Best. Taking the Bishop would enable the Kt. to retreat to an advantageous square.

(*c*) We would have preferred 15. P. x Kt., as it plants the Pawn in a good position, and leaves more pieces with which to operate. The move in the text looks *drawish.*

(*d*) The aspect of the game now becomes decidedly drawish.

(*e*) He could do nothing with the R. at R. 8th. In fact the game is drawn by its nature.

(*f*) R. to K. 8th would have been answered by

	43. R. to K. 8th.
44. P. to B. 5th, check.	44. P. x P., check.
45. R. x P.	45. R. x K. P.
46. R. x Q. P., and White has the best of it.	

(*g*) We think Black could here have won, *i. e.* :—

	50. K. to B. 3d.
51. K. to R. 5th. (1)	51. K. to B. 4th.
52. K. to R. 4th.	52. K. to Kt. 3d.
53. K. to Kt. 4th.	53. B. to K. 8th.
54. P. to Q. Kt. 3d.	54. B. to B. 6th.
55. K. to R. 4th.	55. K. to B. 4th.
56. K. to R. 3d.	56. B. to K. 8th.
57. K. to R. 2d.	57. K. to Kt. 5th.
58. K. to Kt. 2d.	58. B. to B. 6th.
59. K. to B. 2d.	59. K. to R. 6th.
60. K. to Kt. sq.	60. K. to Kt. 6th.
61. K. to B. sq.	61. K. to B. 6th.
62. K. to Kt. sq.	62. K. to K. 7th.
63. K. to Kt. 2d.	63. B. to Q. 7th.
64. B. to R. 3d.	64. K. to Q. 8th.
65. K. to Kt. 3d.	65. B. to B. 8th.

And wins.

(1) Or if—

52. K. to R. 6th. (2)	52. K. to Kt. 5th.
53. K. to Kt. 6th.	53. K. to B. 6th.
54. K. to B. 6th.	54. K. to K. 7th.
55. P. to Kt. 3d.	55. B. to B. 7th.
56. B. to R. 3d.	56. K. to Q. 8th.
57. K. x P.	57. B. to B. 8th.
58. B. x B.	58. K. x B.
59. P. to B. 5th.	59. K. to Q. 7th.
60. P. to B. 6th.	60. P. Queens.
61. P. to B. 7th.	61. Q. to Q. B. sq., check.
62. K. to K. 7th.	62. K. x K. P.

And wins.

(2) Or if—

52. K. to Kt. 3d.	52. K. to K. 2d.
53. K. to B. 2d.	53. K. to Q. 3d.
54. P. to Kt. 3d.	54. K. to B. 3d.
55. K. to K. 2d.	55. B. to B. 6th.
56. B. to R. 3d.	56. K. to Kt. 4th.
57. K. to B. 2d.	57. B. to Q. 7th.
58. K. to K. 2d.	58. P. Queens.
59. B. x Q.	59. B. x B.
60. K. to B. 2d.	60. K. to Kt. 5th.

And wins.

GAME No. 41.

Played on August 25th, 1876, commencing at 9 A. M.

TIME, 4 HOURS.

French Defence.

White (Mr. Elson).	*Black* (Mr. Mason).
1. P. to K. 4th.	1. P. to K. 3d.
2. P. to Q. 4th.	2. P. to Q. 4th.
3. Kt. to Q. B. 3d.	3. Kt. to K. B. 3d.
4. P. x P.	4. P. x P.
5. B. to Q. 3d.	5. B. to Q. 3d.
6. Kt. to B. 3d.	6. Castles.
7. Castles.	7. B. to K. Kt. 5th.
8. B. to K. Kt. 5th.	8. Q. Kt. to Q. 2d. (*a*)
9. Kt. x Q. P.	9. P. to Q. B. 3d.
10. Kt. x Kt., check.	10. Kt. x Kt.
11. P. to Q. B. 3d.	11. P. to K. R. 3d.
12. B. to R. 4th.	12. P. to K. Kt. 4th.
13. B. to Kt. 3d.	13. Kt. to R. 4th.
14. P. to K. R. 3d.	14. B. x Kt.
15. Q. x B.	15. Kt. to Kt. 2d.
16. Q. R. to K. sq.	16. P. to K. B. 4th.
17. B. to K. 5th.	17. Q. to Q. 2d.
18. B. x Kt.	18. K. x B.
19. R. to K. 3d.	19. R. to K. B. 3d.
20. K. R. to K. sq.	20. Q. R. to K. B.
21. R. from K. 3d to K. 2d.	21. Q. to K. B. 2d.

White (MR. ELSON).	*Black* (MR. MASON).
22. P. to Q. Kt. 3d.	22. Q. to K. Kt. 3d.
23. P. to Q. B. 4th.	23. P. to Q. Kt. 3d.
24. P. to Q. 5th.	24. P. to B. 4th.
25. R. to K. 6th.	25. B. to Q. Kt. sq.
26. R. x R.	26. Q. x R.
27. Q. to K. 3d. (*b*)	27. B. to Q. 3d.
28. Q. to K. 6th.	28. R. to B. 2d.
29. Q. x Q., check. (*c*)	29. R. x Q.
30. P. to K. Kt. 4th.	30. P. x P.
31. P. x P.	31. K. to B. 2d.
32. B. to B. 5th.	32. B. to B. 5th.
33. R. to Q. Kt.	33. K. to K. 2d.

Drawn.

NOTES BY JACOB ELSON.

(*a*) A papable slip.

(*b*) White, who up to this point has played faultlessly, now misses his way. By playing R. to Q. 6th he would have improved his position so much as to make victory almost certain. For instance—

27. R. to K. 6th.	27. Q. to R. 8th, check.

(Or Q. to B. 2d. White makes the winning reply of Q. to K. 2d.)

28. B. to B.	28. R. to B. 3d.

(Or Q. x R. P. White wins by Q. to R. 5th.)

29. R. to K. 7th, check.	29. K. to Kt 3d.
30. R. to Q. Kt. 7th.	30. Q. to K. 4th.
31. P. to Kt. 3d.	31. B. to Q. 3d.

White can now reply with R. x R. P., having two clear Pawns more, or play B. to Q. 3d, following the move with P. to K. Kt. 4th, and ought to win easily in either case.

(*c*) This only draws the game.

GAME No. 42.

Played on August 25th, 1876, commencing at 9 A. M.

TIME, 2 HOURS 30 MINUTES.

Center Counter Gambit.

White (MR. ROBERTS).	*Black* (MR. WARE).
1. P. to K. 4th.	1. P. to Q. 4th. (*a*)
2. P. x P.	2. Q. x P.
3. P. to Q. 4th.	3. B. to B. 4th. (*b*)
4. P. to Q. B. 4th.	4. Q. to Q. 2d.
5. B. to K. 3d. (*c*)	5. P. to Q. B. 3d.
6. Q. to Kt. 3d.	6. P. to K. 3d.
7. Q. Kt. to B. 3d.	7. Kt. to K. B. 3d.
8. Q. R. to Q. sq.	8. B. to K. 2d.
9. Kt. to K. B. 3d.	9. Castles.
10. B. to K. 2d. (*d*)	10. Q. to B. 2d.
11. Kt. to K. R. 4th.	11. B. to Kt. 5th.
12. P. to K. B. 3d.	12. B. to R. 4th.
13. P. to K. Kt. 4th. (*e*)	13. Kt. x Kt. P.
14. P. x Kt.	14. B. x Kt., check.
15. K. to Q. 2d.	15. B. to Kt. 3d.
16. Q. R. to K. B. sq.	16. B. to K. 2d. (*f*)
17. P. to K. R. 4th.	17. P. to K. B. 3d.
18. P. to Q. B. 5th.	18. B. to B. 2d.
19. B. to Q. B. 4th.	19. Q. to Q. 2d.
20. P. to Q. R. 4th. (*g*)	20. B. x B. P.
21. K. to B. 2d.	21. B. to Q. Kt. 3d. (*h*)

White (Mr. Roberts).	*Black* (Mr. Ware).
22. P. to K. Kt. 5th.	22. P. to K. B. 4th.
23. P. to R. 5th.	23. P. to K. 4th. (*i*)
24. P. x P.	24. Q. B. x B.
25. Q. x B., check.	25. K. to R. sq.
26. P. to K. 6th. (*j*)	26. Q. to K. 2d.
27. B. x B.	27. P. x B.
28. P. to K. R. 6th.	28. Kt. to R. 3d.
29. Q. R. to K. Kt. sq. (*k*)	29. P. to Kt. 3d.
30. Q. to Q. 4th, check.	30. K. to Kt. sq.
31. Q. x Kt. P. (*l*)	31. Kt. to Kt. 5th, check.
32. K. to Kt. sq.	32. P. to B. 4th.
33. Q. R. to Q. sq.!	33. R. to R. 3d. (*m*)
34. R. to Q. 7th.	34. Q. x R.
35. Q. x R.	35. Q. to B. 3d. (*n*)
36. Q. x Q.	36. Kt. x Q.
37. Kt. to Q. 5th.	37. K. to R. sq.
38. Kt. to B. 6th. (*o*)	38. R. to Q. sq.
39. R. to K. sq.	39. Kt. to K. 2d.
40. K. to B. 2d.	40. P. to K. B. 5th. (*p*)
41. R. to Q. sq.	41. R. to Q. 5th.
42. R. x R.	42. P. x R.
43. K. to Q. 3d.	43. P. to B. 6th.
44. P. to Q. Kt. 4th.	44. Kt. to B. 3d.
45. P. to Kt. 5th.	45. P. to B. 7th.
46. K. to K. 2d.	46. P. to Q. 6th, check.
47. K. x B. P.	47. P. to Q. 7th.
48. K. to K. 2d.	48. Kt. to Q. 5th, check.
49. K. x P.	49. Kt. x P. (*q*)
50. P. to R. 5th.	50. Kt. to B. 2d.
51. P. to R. 6th.	

And Mr. Ware resigned. (*r*)

13*

NOTES BY W. H. SAYEN.

(*a*) The *Handbuch* considers this a bad move, and contends that White has the advantage in every variation.

(*b*) Here the authorities give 3. Q. to K. 5th, check, followed by 4. P. to K. 4th, or 4. B. to B. 4th, but in all cases White has the best of it.

(*c*) 5. Kt. to K. B. 3d, or 5. Kt. to Q. B. 3d, followed by 6. B. to K. 2d, would perhaps have been stronger, threatening to play Kt. to R. 4th, and after exchanging the Kt. for the Q. B., then plant the K. B. at K. B. 3d.

(*d*) Kt. to K. R. 4th might have resulted better, for instance:—

10. Kt. to K. R. 4th.	10. Kt. to Q. R. 3d.
11. Kt. x B.	11. P. x Kt.
12. B. to Q. 3d.	12. P. to Q. Kt. 3d.
13. B. to Q. Kt. sq.	13. Q. R. to Q. sq.
14. Castles.	14. P. to K. Kt. 3d.

15. P. to K. B. 3d, and we prefer White's position.

(*e*) White gives up the Pawn, and retreats his King into safe quarters on the Q. side. The attack obtained seems to have somewhat compensated for the loss of the Pawn.

(*f*) Perhaps it would have been better to retain the B. at R. 5th to retard the advance of the K. R. P., and played instead 16. Q. Kt. to R. 3d, followed by 17. Q. R. to Q. sq.

(*g*) We believe White here intended to play 20. K. to B. 2d, but transposed the moves.

(*h*) He could not safely have taken the Q. P. with B., *i. e.*—

	21. B. x Q. P.
22. B. x B.	22. Q. x B.

23 Q. x Q. Kt. P., and a good game.

(*i*) A bad move, which Mr. Roberts at once takes advantage of in his most brilliant style.

(*j*) Well played!

(*k*) Threatening 30. P. x P., check, followed by P. to Kt. 6th.

(*l*). Again correctly played.

(*m*) Q. R. to Q. sq. would have been better.

(*n*) If 36. Q. to K. 2d, White answers 37. Q. to Kt. 6th, and again threatens R. to Q. sq.

(*o*) The Black King is now hermetically sealed.

(*p*) His game is evidently lost, but Black struggles gallantly to the end, and the game from this point is a fine study.

(*q*) All this is very fine play

(*r*) If P. x P. then 52. P. to Kt. 6th, and if 51. Kt. x Kt. P., then 52. P. x Kt. P., or if—

	51. P. to Kt. 3d.
52. P. to R. 7th.	52. Kt. to R. 8th.
53. K. to Q. 3d.	

And brings the K. up to Q. B. 6th, and then plays the Kt. to Q. 5th and wins. This game is finely played from the 25th move by Mr. Roberts.

GAME No. 43.

Played on August 25th, 1876, commencing at 9 A.M.

TIME, 4 HOURS 30 MINUTES.

King's Bishop's Gambit.

White (Mr. Mason).	*Black* (Mr. Davidson).
1. P. to K. 4th.	1. P. to K. 4th.
2. P. to K. B. 4th.	2. P. x P.
3. B. to B. 4th.	3. K. Kt. to B. 3d. (*a*)
4. Q. to K. 2d. (*b*)	4. P. to Q. 3d.
5. P. to Q. 4th.	5. B. to Kt. 5th.
6. K. Kt. to B. 3d.	6. P. to K. Kt. 4th.
7. P. to K. R. 4th.	7. Kt. to R. 4th.
8. Q. to Q. 3d.	8. Kt. to Kt. 6th.
9. R. to R. 2d.	9. P. to K. B. 3d. (*c*)
10. Q. Kt. to B. 3d.	10. P. to Q. B. 3d.
11. B. to Q. 2d. (*d*)	11. Kt. to Q. 2d.
12. Castles.	12. B. to K. 2d.
13. P. x P.	13. P. x P.
14. P. to Q. 5th.	14. B. x Kt.
15. P. x B.	15. Kt. to K. 4th. (*e*)
16. Q. to Q. 4th.	16. P. to B. 4th.
17. B. to Kt. 5th, check.	17. K. to B. 2d.
18. Q. to B. 2d.	18. P. to K. R. 4th.
19. B. to B. sq.	19. P. to R. 5th.
20. B. to R. 3d.	20. R. to Q. Kt. sq.
21. B. to K. 6th, check.	21. K. to Kt. 2d.

White (Mr. Mason).	*Black* (Mr. Davidson).
22. Kt. to K. 2d.	22. P. to Kt. 4th.
23. K. to Kt. sq.	23. Kt. to B. 5th.
24. B. x P. (*f*)	24. P. x B.
25. Kt. x P.	25. B. to Kt. 4th.
26. Kt. to Q. 3d.	26. B. to K. 6th.
27. Q. to Kt. 2d.	27. Q. to B. 3d. (*g*)
28. K. to R. sq.	28. Kt. to K. 4th.
29. Kt. x Kt.	29. Q. x Kt.
30. R. to Q. 3d.	30. Q. to B. 5th.
31. R. to R. sq.	31. P. to B. 5th.
32. R. to Q. R. 3d.	32. P. to Kt. 5th.
33. R. to R. 6th.	33. Q. R. to K. B. sq. (*h*)
34. R. to B. 6th.	34. B. to Kt. 3d.
35. R. to K. sq.	35. Q. x B. P.
36. Q. to Q. 2d.	36. Kt. x. P.
37. Q. x Q. Kt. P.	37. P. to R. 6th. (*i*)
38. R. x B. P.	38. R. to R. 5th.
39. B. x P.	39. B. to B. 4th.
40. Q. to R. 4th.	40. Q. to Kt. 6th.
41. R. fr. B. 4th x Kt. (*j*)	41. Q. x R., check.
42. R. x Q.	42. R. x Q.

And Mr. Mason resigned.

NOTES BY W. H. SAYEN.

(*a*) See game between Bird and Mason.

(*b*) Obsolete, and now seldom played. Not so strong as Kt. to Q. B. 3d.

(*c*) Black intends to hold the gambit pawn, and this is much the best move to do so. It also frees the action of the King.

(*d*) Preparatory to Castling on the Queen's side.

(*e*) Planting this Kt. in a fine position, which becomes very annoying to White. In fact, the defence is now with the first player.

(*f*) This sacrifice was made to relieve his game from two of the dangerous pawns, and, at the same time, he had only the choice of exchanging the Bishop, or submitting to the attack of B. to K. B. 3d, and the fatal posting of the Kt. at Q. R. 6th. The move in the text also gives possibilities for a counter attack in the near future.

(*g*) We think Mr. Davidson had a much better line of play in the following:—

	27. B. to Q. 5th.
28. R. to Q. B. sq.	28. P. to Q. Kt. 5th.
29. Q. to K. R. 3d.	29. Q. to K. B. 3d.
30. Q. to Kt. 4th, check.	30. K. to B. sq.
31. Q. to B. 4th.	31. B. x Q. Kt. P.
32. R. to K. Kt. sq.	32. Q. x Q.
33. Kt. x Q.	33. B. to Q. 5th.
34. Kt. to Kt. 6th, check.	34. K. to Kt. 2d.

And Black wins.

(*h*) We would here prefer 33. B. to Q. Kt. 3d most decidedly. It completely isolates the Q. R., besides opening on the next move with 34. Q. R. to K. B. sq., and the defence of the K. B. P. becomes impossible.

(*i*) This loses the Pawn. 37. R. to K. R. 4th seems preferable, as it frees the King, and also the action of the K. B., and if White now play 38. R. x Q. B. P., Black answers 38. B. to Q. B. 4th, compelling an exchange of Queens, or else driving the White Queen out of play, *i. e.*:—

	37. R. to K. R. 4th.
38. R. x Q. B. P.	38. B. to B. 4th.
39. Q. to Kt. 7th, check.	39. K. to R. sq.

And, as the Kt. cannot evidently be captured, the advance of the R. P. becomes irresistible, for if 40. P. to Q. Kt. 4th, Black answers 40. R. to K. R. 2d.

(*j*) A misconception of the position, which loses at once. 41. Q. to R. 4th seems to have been the only move.

GAME No. 44.

Played on August 26th, 1876, commencing at 11 A. M.

TIME, 2 HOURS.

Sicilian Defence.

White (Mr. Elson).	*Black* (Mr. Barbour).
1. P. to K. 4th.	1. P. to K. 3d.
2. P. to Q. 4th.	2. P. to Q. B. 4th.
3. Kt. to K. B. 3d.	3. P. x P.
4. Kt. x P.	4. Kt. to Q. B. 3d.
5. B. to K. 3d.	5. K. Kt. to K. 2d.
6. B. to Q. 3d.	6. Kt. x Kt.
7. B. x Kt.	7. Kt. to Q. B. 3d.
8. B. to Q. B. 3d.	8. B. to Q. Kt. 5th.
9. Castles.	9. B. x B.
10. Kt. x B.	10. Castles.
11. K. to R. sq.	11. Kt. to K. 4th.
12. B. to K. 2d.	12. P. to K. B. 4th.
13. P. to K. B. 4th.	13. Kt. to Q. B. 3d.
14. P. to K. 5th. (*a*)	14. P. to Q. R. 3d.
15. Q. to Q. 2d.	15. P. to Q. Kt. 4th.
16. Q. R. to Q. sq.	16. R. to Q. Kt. sq.
17. B. to K. B. 3d.	17. Kt. to K. 2d.
18. Kt. to K. 2d.	18. P. to K. R. 3d.
19. Kt. to Q. 4th.	19. B. to Kt. 2d. (*b*)

White (Mr. Elson).	*Black* (Mr. Barbour).
20. B. x B.	20. R. x B.
21. Kt. x K. P.	21. P. x Kt.
22. Q. x Q.	22. R. x Q.
23. R. x R., check.	23. K. to B. 2d.
24. R. to Q. 6th.	24. P. to Q. R. 4th.
25. P. to Q. B. 3d.	25. Kt. to Q. 4th.
26. R. to Q. sq.	26. R. to Q. B. 2d.
27. P. to K. Kt. 3d.	27. K. to K. 2d.
28. R. x Kt.	28. P. x R.
29. R. x P.	29. P. to Kt. 5th.
30. R. x R. P.	30. P. x P.
31. P. x P.	31. R. x P.
32. R. to R. 7th, check.	32. K. to K. 3d.
33. R. x Kt. P.	33. K. to Q. 4th.
34. K. to Kt. 2d.	34. R. to B. 7th, check.
35. K. to R. 3d.	35. R. x Q. R. P.
36. R. to Kt. 6th.	36. P. to R. 4th.
37. R. to Kt. 5th.	37. K. to K. 5th.
38. R. x R. P.	38. R. to R. 3d.
39. K. to R. 4th.	39. R. to R. 7th.
40. K. to Kt. 5th.	40. R. to R. sq.
41. R. to R. 6th.	41. R. to K. Kt. sq., check.
42. R. to K. Kt. 6th.	42. R. to Q. R. sq.
43. P. to K. 6th.	43. R. to K. sq.
44. K. to B. 6th.	44. R. to B. sq., check.
45. K. to K. 7th.	45. R. to Q. R. sq.
46. K. to B. 7th.	46. R. to K. R. sq.
47. P. to K. 7th.	47. R. to R. 2d, check.
48. R. to Kt. 7th.	Resigns.

NOTES BY JACOB ELSON.

(*a*) The position of White's Pawns is now greatly superior to those of Black.

(*b*) P. to Q. 4th would have been replied to with P. x P. in passing, and on Q. x P., Kt. x K. B. P. The correct move was Q. to K. sq., but in any case the game was much in favor of White.

GAME No. 45.

Played on August 26th, 1876, commencing at 2 P. M.

TIME, 1 HOUR 30 MINUTES.

Petroff's Defence.

White (MR. BARBOUR).	*Black* (MR. ELSON).
1. P. to K. 4th.	1. P. to K. 4th.
2. Kt. to K. B. 3d.	2. Kt. to K. B. 3d.
3. P. to Q. 4th.	3. Kt. x K. P. (*a*)
4. B. to Q. 3d.	4. P. to Q. 4th.
5. Kt. x K. P.	5. B. to K. 2d.
6. Castles.	6. Castles.
7. P. to Q. B. 4th.	7. Kt. to K. B. 3d.
8. P. to Q. B. 5th. (*b*)	8. Kt. to Q. B. 3d.
9. Kt. x Kt.	9. P. x Kt.
10. P. to K. R. 3d.	10. Kt. to K. 5th.
11. R. to K. sq.	11. P. to K. B. 4th.
12. B. to K. B. 4th.	12. B to Kt. 4th.
13. B. to K. 5th.	13. B. to B. 3d.
14. P. to K. B. 3d.	14. B. x B. (*c*)
15. P. x B.	15. Kt. x Q. B. P.
16. P. to K. B. 4th.	16. Q. to K. R. 5th.
17. R. to B. sq.	17. P. to Q. R. 4th.
18. K. to R. 2d. (*d*)	18. Kt. x B.
19. Q. x Kt.	19. B. to R. 3d.
20. Q. to K. B. 3d.	20. B. x R.
21. Q. x B.	21. Q. R. to Q. Kt.

White (Mr. Barbour).	*Black* (Mr. Elson).
22. P. to K. Kt. 3d. (*e*)	22. R. x Kt. P., check.
23. K. to R. sq.	23. Q. x K. Kt. P.
Resigns.	

NOTES BY JACOB ELSON.

(*a*) P. x P. is considered the better move.

(*b*) By no means commendable. B. to K. 3d, Kt. to Q. B. 3d, or P. x P. were either of them to be preferred.

(*c*) Winning at least a P.

(*d*) Completely oblivious of Black's object in advancing the Q. R. P.

(*e*) The game being past recovery, it was immaterial what he played.

GAME No. 46.

Played on August 26th, 1876, commencing at 9 A. M.

TIME, 8 HOURS 30 MINUTES.

Ruy Lopez's Knight's Game.

White (MR. DAVIDSON).	*Black* (MR. MASON).
1. P. to K. 4th.	1. P. to K. 4th.
2. Kt. to K. B. 3d.	2. Q. Kt. to B. 3d.
3. B. to Kt. 5th.	3. Kt. to Q. 5th. (*a*)
4. Kt. x Kt.	4. P. x Kt.
5. P. to Q. 3d.	5. B. to B. 4th. (*b*)
6. Castles. (*c*)	6. P. to Q. B. 3d.
7. B. to B. 4th.	7. P. to Q. 3d.
8. P. to Q. B. 3d.	8. Q. to B. 3d.
9. K. to R. sq.	9. P. to K. R. 4th.
10. P. to K. B. 4th.	10. B. to K. Kt. 5th.
11. Q. to K. sq.	11. Q. to K. 2d.
12. Kt. to Q. 2d.	12. Kt. to B. 3d.
13. P. to Q. R. 4th.	13. P. to R. 5th.
14. Kt. to Kt. 3d.	14. P. x P.
15. P. x P.	15. B. to Kt. 3d.
16. P. to R. 5th. (*d*)	16. B. to B. 2d.
17. B. to K. 3d.	17. Kt. to R. 4th.
18. K. to Kt. sq.	18. P. to Q. R. 3d.
19. Kt. to Q. 4th.	19. P. to R. 6th.
20. P. to Kt. 3d.	20. R. to Q. sq.
21. Q. to B. 2d.	21. Castles.

White (Mr. Davidson).	*Black* (Mr. Mason).
22. Kt. to B. 3d.	22. K. R. to K. sq.
23. K. R. to K. sq.	23. Q. to Q. 2d.
24. B. to Kt. 3d.	24. Kt. to B. 3d.
25. Kt. to Kt. 5th.	25. P. to Q. 4th.
26. B. to Q. 4th. (*e*)	26. Kt. to R. 2d.
27. Kt. to B. 3d.	27. P. to B. 3d.
28. B. to B. 5th.	28. K. to R. sq.
29. Kt. to R. 4th.	29. B. to R. 4th.
30. P. x P.	30. P. x P.
31. R. x R., check.	31. Q. x R.
32. B. to R. 4th.!	32. Q. to K. 7th.
33. Q. x Q.	33. B. x Q.
34. B. to K. 7th.	34. R. to Q. Kt. sq.
35. P. to Q. 4th. (*f*)	35. P. to K. Kt. 4th.
36. Kt. to Kt. 6th, check.	36. K. to Kt. 2d.
37. B. to B. 2.	37. B. to R. 4th.
38. P. to B. 5th.	38. P. to Kt. 5th.
39. B. to Kt. 3d. (*g*)	39. B. x Kt.
40. P. x B.	40. K. x P.
41. B. x Q. P.	41. Kt. to Kt. 4th.
42. B. to B. 5th. (*h*)	42. P. to B. 4th.
43. B. to R. 7th.	43. R. to K. sq.
44. B. to Kt. 6th. (*i*)	44. B. x B.
45. P. x B.	45. Kt. to B. 6th, check.
46. B. x Kt.	46. P. x B.
47. K. to B. 2d.	47. R. to K. 7th, check.
48. K. x P.	48. R. to Q. Kt. 7th.
49. P. to Kt. 4th.	49. R. x Kt. P.
50. P. x P., check.	50. K. x P.
51. R. to R. 5th, check.	51. K. to K. 3d.
52. K. to Kt. 4th.	52. R. to Kt. 6th.
53. R. to B. 5th. (*j*)	53. P. to Kt. 3d.

White (Mr. Davidson).	*Black* (Mr. Mason).
54. R. to K. R. 5th.	54. R. x P.
55. R. to R. 6th, check.	55. K. to Q. 4th.
56. R. x Kt. P.	56. R. to R. 6th.
57. R. to Kt. 8th.	57. K. x P.
58. R. to Q. 8th, check.	58. K. to B. 4th.
59. R. to B. 8th, check.	59. K. to Kt. 5th.
60. R. to Kt. 8th, check.	60. K. to R. 5th.
61. R. to K. R. 8th.	61. P. to R. 4th.

And Mr. Davidson resigned.

NOTES BY W. H. SAYEN.

(*a*) This move, much affected by Mr. Bird in America, and played by him in the Vienna Tourney, is not good in our opinion, when correctly answered, *i. e.* :—

5. P. to Q. 3d. !	5. B. to Q. B. 4th.
6. Q. to R. 5th.	6. Q. to K. 2d.
7. B. to Kt. 5th.	7. B. to Kt. 5th, check.
8. P. to Q. B. 3d.	8. Q. P. x P.
9. Kt. P. x P.	9. Q. to Q. B. 4th.
10. B. to Q. B. 4th.	10. P. to K. Kt. 3d.
11. Q. to K. B. 3d.	11. Q. x Q. B.
12. Q. x K. B. P., check.	12. K. to Q. sq.
13. P. x K. B., and wins.	

If Black play 5. P. to Q. B. 3d, White plays B. to B. 4th, and obtains a fine game.

(*b*) Not so good as P. to Q. B. 3d, yet, even in that event, Black retreats the B. to B. 4th, and obtains a strong centre.

(*c*) Not so good as Q. to R. 5th, which, with the most careful play on both sides, as above demonstrated, gives White the advantage.

(*d*) This Pawn now becomes weak, and the move is not to be commended. 16. P. to K. R. 3d could have been played, as the sacrifice of the Bishop would not have been sound, and the

Bishop must retreat on the B. file, and then 17. Kt. to Q. 2d, followed by 18. Kt. to K. B. 3d gives a fine game.

(*e*) The following appears to be better :—

26. P. to K. 5th.	26. Kt. to R. 2d.
27. Kt. x Kt.	27. K. x Kt.
28. P. to Q. 4th, with the better game.	

(*f*) Here White could have obtained a decided advantage, we think, by the following line of play :—

35. Kt. to Kt. 6th, check.	35. K. to Kt. sq.
36. B. to Kt. 3d.	36. K. to B. 2d, best.
37. P. to K. B. 5th.	37. B. x Q. P., best.
38. B. x Q. P., check.	38. K. to K. sq.
39. P. to Kt. 4th.	39. Kt. to Kt. 4th.
40. R. to K. sq.	

And we cannot see how Black can escape without serious loss.

(*g*) Probably the best move.

(*h*) Here we would much prefer 39. K. to B. 2d, for if—

	39. R. to K. sq.
40. B. to B. 5th.	40. Kt. to K. 5th, check.
41. B. x Kt., check.	41. R. x B.
42. B. to Kt. 4th.	42. P. to B. 4th.
43. P. to Q. 5th.	43. B. to K. 4th.
44. R. to Q. sq.	44. P. to B. 5th.
45. P. to Q. 6th.	45. P. x P., check.
46. P. x P.	46. B. to B. 3d.
47. R. to Q. 5th.	

And the game is at least equal.

(*i*) He dared not capture the Pawn on account of the reply, 44. P. to B. 5th.

(*j*) Bad judgment. He could only hope for a draw, and K. x P. would have given him the best chance.

GAME No. 47.

Played on August 28th, 1876, commencing at 9 A.M.

TIME, 4 HOURS.

Ruy Lopez's Knight's Game.

White (Mr. Elson).	*Black* (Mr. Judd).
1. P. to K. 4th.	1. P. to K. 4th.
2. Kt. to K. B. 3d.	2. Kt. to Q. B. 3d.
3. B. to Kt. 5th.	3. Kt. to K. 2d. (*a*)
4. Castles.	4. P. to K. Kt. 3d.
5. P. to Q. B. 3d. (*b*)	5. B. to Kt. 2d.
6. P. to Q. 4th.	6. P. x P.
7. P. x P.	7. P. to Q. R. 3d.
8. B. to R. 4th.	8. P. to Q. Kt. 4th.
9. B. to Kt. 3d.	9. P. to Q. 3d.
10. P. to K. R. 3d.	10. Castles.
11. Q. to Kt. B. 3d.	11. B. to Kt. 2d.
12. Q. B. to Kt. 5th.	12. P. to K. R. 3d.
13. B. to K. 3d.	13. K. to R. 2d.
14. B. to B. 2d.	14. P. to K. B. 4th.
15. Kt. to K. 2d.	15. Kt. to Kt. 5th.
16. Kt. to Q. 2d. (*c*)	16. Kt. x B.
17. Q. x Kt.	17. P. x P.
18. Kt. x P.	18. Kt. to Q. 4th.
19. K. Kt. to Kt. 3d.	19. Q. to R. 5th.
20. Q. R. to K. sq.	20. Q. R. to K. sq.
21. B. to B. sq. (*d*)	21. B. x Q. P.

White (Mr. Elson).	*Black* (Mr. Judd).
22. R. to K. 2d.	22. R. to K. 2d.
23. Kt. to Kt. 5th, ch. (*e*)	23. P. x Kt.
24. R. x R., check.	24. Kt. x R.
25. Q. x B. P.	25. R. to B. 2d.
26. Q. x B.	26. Q. x Kt.
27. Q. to K. 4th.	27. R. x B. P.
28. R. x R.	28. Q. x R., check.
	And wins.

NOTES BY JACOB ELSON.

(*a*) This defence is justly condemned.

(*b*) P. to Q. 4th is the correct move.

(*c*) P. x P. was obviously the correct move, and would have given White a fine attack.

(*d*) Curiously enough, White is compelled to retreat this B. and give up Q. P., or lose a piece.

(*e*) In making this combination White overlooked the fact that after the capture of B. with Q., at move 26, the Kt. would be en prise by the Q., as the B. pinned the K. B. P. Black, however, had any way much the best of it.

GAME No. 48.

Played on August 28th, 1876, commencing at 6 P. M.

TIME, 4 HOURS.

Stein Opening.

White (Mr. Judd).	*Black* (Mr. Elson).
1. P. to Q. 4th.	1. P. to K. B. 4th.
2. P. to K. 4th.	2. P. x P.
3. Q. Kt. to B. 3d.	3. K. Kt. to B. 3d.
4. Q. B. to Kt. 5th.	4. P. to K. 3d.
5. Kt. x P.	5. B. to K. 2d.
6. Kt. x Kt., check.	6. B. x Kt.
7. B. to K. 3d.	7. Castles.
8. Kt. to B. 3d.	8. P. to Q. Kt. 3d.
9. B. to K. 2d.	9. B. to Kt. 2d.
10. Castles.	10. P. to Q. 3d.
11. P. to Q. B. 3d.	11. K. to R. sq.
12. Q. to B. 2d.	12. Q. to K. sq.
13. Kt. to Q. 2d.	13. Kt. to Q. 2d.
14. Kt. to K. 4th.	14. Q. to Kt. 3d.
15. B. to Q. 3d.	15. Q. to R. 4th.
16. P. to K. B. 3d.	16. B. x Kt.
17. B. x B.	17. P. to Q. 4th.
18. B. to Q. 3d.	18. B. to K. 2d.
19. P. to K. B. 4th.	19. Kt. to B. 3d.
20. R. to B. 3d.	20. Kt. to Kt. 5th.
21. R. to R. 3d.	21. Kt. x B.

White (Mr. Judd).	*Black* (Mr. Elson).
22. R. x Q.	22. Kt. x Q.
23. B. x R. P. (*a*)	23. Kt. x R.
24. B. to B. 5th, check.	24. K. to Kt.
25. B. x P., check.	25. R. to B. 2d.
26. P. to B. 5th.	26. R. to Q.
27. K. to B. 2d.	27. Kt. to B. 7th.
28. K. to K. 2d.	28. R. to Q. 3d.
29. B. x R., check.	29. K. x B.
30. K. to Q. 2d.	30. Kt. x P.
31. P. x Kt.	31. R. to R. 3d.
32. R. x R.	32. P. x R. (*b*)

The game was finally drawn.

NOTES BY JACOB ELSON.

(*a*) Played under the incredible misconception that he could force mate with the R. and the B.!

(*b*) Black here has of course an easily won game, but by a slip he lost the B., and finally only succeeded in drawing. In order to have the matter more fully understood, however, it is but proper to mention that Black, being seriously indisposed that day, begged to be excused from playing till the next day. White declining to grant that request, lots were drawn, which decided that Black had to play that day. White, instead of resigning at this point a *dead lost game*, held on to it, and finally succeeded in drawing.

GAME No. 49.

Played on August 28th, 1876, commencing at 9 A. M.

TIME, 1 HOUR 50 MINUTES.

Ruy Lopez Knight's Game.

White (MR. DAVIDSON).	*Black* (MR. BIRD).
1. P. to K. 4th.	1. P. to K. 4th.
2. K. Kt. to B. 3d.	2. Q. Kt. to B. 3d.
3. B. to Kt. 5th.	3. Kt. to Q. 5th. (*a*)
4. Kt. x Kt.	4. P. x Kt.
5. P. to Q. 3d.	5. B. to B. 4th.
6. Castles. (*b*)	6. P. to Q. B. 3d.
7. K. B. to B. 4th.	7. P. to Q. 4th.
8. P. x P.	8. P. x P.
9. B. to Kt. 5th, check. (*c*)	9. K. to B. sq. (*d*)
10. Q. B. to B. 4th.	10. P. to K. R. 4th.
11. R. to K. sq.	11. Kt. to K. 2d.
12. Kt. to Q. 2d.	12. B. to K. Kt. 5th.
13. P. to K. B. 3d.	13. B. to K. 3d.
14. Kt. to Kt. 3d.	14. B. to Kt. 3d.
15. B. to Kt. 5th.	15. Q. to Q. 3d.
16. B. x Kt., check.	16. Q. x B.
17. P. to Q. R. 4th. (*e*)	17. P. to R. 3d.
18. P. to R. 5th.	18. B. to B. 2d.
19. B. to R. 4th.	19. Q. to Q. 3d.
20. P. to Kt. 3d.	20. P. to R. 5th.
21. P. to B. 4th.	21. P. x P.

White (Mr. Davidson).	*Black* (Mr. Bird).
22. P. x P.	22. P. to K. Kt. 4th.
23. Kt. x Q. P. (*f*)	23. P. x P.
24. Kt. x B., check.	24. P. x Kt.
25. R. to K. 2d.	25. P. to B. 6th.
White resigns.	

NOTES BY B. M. NEILL.

(*a*) This move, although generally considered an inferior one, is very formidable in the hands of Mr. Bird, he being well versed in the variations arising therefrom.

(*b*) Q. to R. 5th seems a strong method of continuing the attack.

(*c*) There seems to be little gained by this check, as Black does not intend to Castle. B. to Kt. 3d was better.

(*d*) Correctly played.

(*e*) We now see the bad results of White's 9th move. His B. is not only out of play, but he is compelled to make this otherwise useless move to save a piece.

(*f*) White's game is hopeless. Mr. Bird finishes it in the same excellent style he has exhibited all through.

GAME No. 50.

Played on August 28th, 1876, commencing at 9 A.M.

TIME, 1 HOUR.

Scotch Gambit.

White (Mr. Judd).	*Black* (Mr. Roberts).
1. P. to K. 4th.	1. P. to K. 4th.
2. Kt. to K. B. 3d.	2. Kt. to Q. B. 3d.
3. P. to Q. 4th.	3. P. x P.
4. Kt. x P.	4. Q. to R. 5th.
5. Kt. to K. B. 3d.	5. Q. x P., check.
6. B. to K. 2d.	6. B. to Kt. 5th, check.
7. P. to B. 3d.	7. B. to K. 2d.
8. Castles.	8. P. to Q. Kt. 3d.
9. R. to K. sq.	9. B. to Q. Kt. 2d. (*a*)
10. B. to Q. R. 6th.	10. Q. to Kt. 5th.
11. B. x B.	11. R. to Q. Kt. sq.
12. B. x Kt.	12. P. x B.
13. Kt. to Q. 4th.	13. Q. to Kt. 3d.

And, after a few moves, Black resigned.

NOTE BY W. H. SAYEN.

(*a*) An oversight which loses the game. It is but justice to Mr. Roberts to state that he labored under some indisposition at this time.

GAME No. 51.

Played on August 28th, 1876, commencing at 2.30 P. M.

TIME, 6 HOURS.

King's Gambit Declined.

White (Mr. Roberts).	*Black* (Mr. Judd).
1. P. to K. 4th.	1. P. to K. 4th.
2. P. to K. B. 4th.	2. B. to Q. B. 4th. (*a*)
3. Kt. to K. B. 3d.	3. P. to Q. 3d.
4. P. to Q. B. 3d. (*b*)	4. Kt. to K. B. 3d.
5. P. x P. (*c*)	5. P. x P.
6. Kt. x P.	6. Q. to K. 2d.
7. P. to Q. 4th.	7. B. to Q. 3d.
8. Kt. to B. 3d.	8. Kt. x P.
9. B. to K. 2d.	9. Castles.
10. Castles.	10. P. to K. R. 3d.
11. B. to Q. 3d.	11. K. Kt. to B. 3d.
12. R. to K. sq. (*d*)	12. Q. to Q. sq.
13. Kt. to Q. 2d.	13. P. to Q. B. 3d.
14. Kt. to B. 4th.	14. Q. B. to Kt. 5th. (*e*)
15. P. to K. R. 3d.	15. B. to K. 3d.
16. Q. Kt. to K. 5th.	16. Q. Kt. to Q. 2d.
17. Q. B. to B. 4th.	17. Kt. to Q. 4th. (*f*)
18. Kt. x K. B. P. (*g*)	18. R. x Kt.
19. B. x B.	19. Q. to B. 3d.
20. Kt. to K. 5th. (*h*)	20. Q. to B. 7th, check.
21. K. to R. sq.	21. Kt. to B. 5th.

White (Mr. Roberts).	*Black* (Mr. Judd).
22. B. to K. 4th.	22. Kt. x Kt.
23. B. x Kt.	23. Q. x Kt. P.
24. R. to Q. Kt. sq. (*i*)	24. Q. x R. P.
25. B. x Kt.	25. R. x B.
26. R. x P.	26. Q. R. to K. B. sq.
27. B. x B. P. (*j*)	27. Q. to R. 3d.
28. P. to Q. 5th.	28. B. to B. sq. (*k*)
29. Q. R. to K. 7th. (*l*)	29. Q. to B. 5th.
30. Q. R. to K. 3d.	30. R. to B. 8th, check.
31. K. to R. 2d.	31. Q. to B. 5th, check.
32. R. to Kt. 3d.	32. R. to B. 7th.
33. P. to B. 4th. (*m*)	33. R. x P., check. (*n*)
34. K. x R.	34. Q. to B. 7th, check.
35. K. to R. sq.	35. Q. x R.
36. P. to Q. 6th.	36. R. to B. 7th.
37. Q. to Q. 5th, check.	37. K. to R. 2d.

And Mr. Roberts resigned. (*o*)

NOTES BY W. H. SAYEN.

(*a*) This and 2. P. to Q. 4th, are given as the best moves, when the gambit is declined.

(*b*) Much stronger than 4. B. to Q. B. 4th.

(*c*) Many authorities prefer 5. P. to Q. 4th, *i. e.*:—

5. P. to Q. 4th.	5. K. P. x Q. P.
6. P. x P.	6. B. to Kt. 3d, best.
7. B. to Q. 3d.	7. Castles.
8. Castles.	8. Kt. to Q. B. 3d.
9. B. to K. 3d,	

and White has a strong centre.

(*d*) White has shown great judgment in position in this opening, and his game presents a decidedly better appearance than that of Black. 12. Q. Kt. to Q. 2d, followed by 13. Kt. to B.

4th, also offered inducements, as the R. at K. B. sq. seems to us stronger than at K. sq.

(*e*) Weak. B. to Q. B. 2d, better.

(*f*) An oversight. He should have played, 17. B. to Q. B. 2d.

(*g*) We would much have preferred to capture the valuable Q. B. P. He would also have avoided the harassing attack which resulted from Q. to K. B. 3d.

(*h*) A move representing great depth of combination, and which will repay the closest scrutiny.

(*i*) Well played. All the foregoing five moves have been carefully considered on both sides.

(*j*) We think this capture sound, with the best play, yet it has the disadvantage of shutting a valuable Bishop out of play.

(*k*) He could not play B. x K. R. P., *i. e.*:—

	28. B. x K. R. P.
29. Q. to K. 2d.	29. R. to B. 8th, check.
30. K. to R. 2d.	30. Q. x Q.
31. R. x Q.	31. B. to B. sq.
32. R. x R. P., and wins.	

(*l*) Here White overlooked a much better move, 29. R. to Q. Kt. 4th. The move in the text looks well, but the answer of Q. to Q. B. 5th, completely frustrates its ultimate purposes on the K. Kt. Pawn, *i. e.*:—

29. R. to Q. Kt. 4th.	29. R. to B. 8th, check.
30. K. to R. 2d.	30. R. to B. 7th.
31. P. to Q. B. 4th.	31. Q. to R. 7th.
32. P. to Q. 6th, and wins.	

(*m*) R. to K. Kt. sq. was a good move, or, better, Q. to Q. 4th would have insured an exchange of Queens, besides threatening R. to K. 7th.

(*n*) Mr. Judd plays the remaining moves very skilfully.

(*o*) We repeat that Mr. Roberts was ill during the latter part of this game, and the one previous.

GAME No. 52.

Played on August 29th, 1876, commencing at 9 A. M.

TIME, 4 HOURS.

Queen's Gambit Declined.

White (Mr. Mason).	*Black* (Mr. Ware).
1. P. to Q. 4th.	1. P. to Q. 4th.
2. P. to Q. B. 4th.	2. P. to K. 3d. (*a*)
3. Kt. to K B. 3d.	3. P. to Q. B. 3d. (*b*)
4. Kt. to Q. B. 3d.	4. P. to K. B. 4th. (*c*)
5. B. to B. 4th.	5. Kt. to K. B. 3d.
6. P. to K. 3d.	6. B. to K. 2d. (*d*)
7. B. to Q. 3d.	7. Castles.
8. Castles.	8. B. to Q. 3d.
9. B. x B.	9. Q. x B.
10. Kt. to K. 5th.	10. Q. Kt. to Q. 2d.
11. P. to K. B. 4th.	11. Q. to K. 2d.
12. P. x P.	12. B. P. x P.
13. Q. to K. 2d.	13. Kt. x Kt.
14. B. P. x Kt.	14. Kt. to K. Kt. 5th.
15. Kt. to Q. Kt. 5th.	15. B. to Q. 2d.
16. Kt. to Q. 6th. (*e*)	16. B. to B. 3d.
17. R. to B. 3d.	17. Q. R. to Q. sq.
18. Q. R. to K. B. sq.	18. P. to K. Kt. 3d.
19. P. to K. R. 3d.	19. Kt. to R. 3d.
20. P. to Q. Kt. 4th.	20. P. to Q. R. 3d.
21. Q. R. to Q. B. sq.	21. Kt. to B. 2d, best.

White (Mr. Mason).	*Black* (Mr. Ware).
22. Kt. x Kt.	22. R. x Kt.
23. B. x R. P. (*f*)	23. Q. x Q. Kt. P.
24. B. to Q. 3d.	24. R. to Q. R. sq.
25. P. to K. Kt. 4th.	25. P. to B. 5th.
26. Q. R. to K. B. sq.	26. Q. R. to K. B. sq.
27. P. to Q. R. 3d.	27. Q. to Kt. 3d. (*g*)
28. K. to R. 2d.	28. P. x P.
29. R. x R.	29. R. x R.
30. R. x R.	30. K. x R.
31. Q. x P.	31. B. to R. 5th. (*h*)
32. P. to K. R. 4th.	32. B. to Q. 8th.
33. K. to Kt. 3d.	33. Q. to Kt. 6th.
34. P. to R. 5th.	34. P. x P. (*i*)
35. P. x P.	35. B. x P.
36. B. to Kt. 6th, check. (*j*)	
And Mr. Ware resigned.	

NOTES BY W. H. SAYEN.

(*a*) Generally regarded as the best move, when the gambit is declined.

(*b*) We prefer 3. Kt. to K. B. 3d, and if 4. B. to Kt. 5th, then 4. B. to K. 2d.

(*c*) Weak. Kt. to K. B. 3d, much better.

(*d*) B. to Q. 3d at once, saves time and is stronger.

(*e*) This Kt., though apparently in a fine position, is harmless to Black's game.

(*f*) White was desirous of breaking up the Q. side. We think Black now gets the best of it.

(*g*) It is evident that if he take the Pawn, he loses the valuable K. B. P.

(*h*) This move occupied one and a half hours. Leading, as it did, to such a fine combination, and losing by such a glaring oversight, when victory was possible, was a misfortune attributable alone to the ill health of the New England champion.

(*i*) Here he should have played K. to Kt. 2d, and it is difficult to see how White can escape loss, as B. to B. 7th is threatened. If 35. K. to B. 2d—B. x Kt. P., etc.

(*j*) Incredible, but nevertheless so.

GAME No. 53.

Played on August 30th, 1876, commencing at 9 A.M.

TIME, 1 HOUR.

French Defence.

White (MR. WARE).	*Black* (MR. MASON).
1. P. to K. 4th.	1. P. to K. 3d.
2. P. to K. B. 4th.	2. P. to Q. 4th.
3. P. to K. 5th.	3. P. to Q. B. 4th.
4. Kt. to K. B. 3d.	4. Kt. to Q. B. 3d.
5. B. to Kt. 5th.	5. P. to Q. R. 4th.
6. B. x Kt., check.	6. P. x B.
7. Castles.	7. Kt. to K. R. 3d.
8. K. to R. sq.	8. B. to Q. R. 3d.
9. P. to Q. 3d.	9. P. to Q. B. 5th.
10. P. to Q. 4th.	10. P. to Q. B. 4th.
11. P. to Q. B. 3d.	11. B. to K. 2d.
12. Kt. to Q. R. 3d.	12. Castles.
13. Kt. to Q. B. 2d.	13. P. to K. B. 4th.
14. P. x P. en pass.	14. K. B. x P.
15. Kt. to K. 5th.	15. Q. to Q. Kt. 3d.
16. P. to Q. R. 3d.	16. B. x Kt.
17. B. P. x B.	17. R. x R., check.
18. Q. x R.	18. R. to K. B. sq.
19. Q. to K. 2d.	19. Kt. to Kt. 5th.
20. P. to K. R. 3d.	20. Kt. to B. 7th, check.
21. K. to R. 2d.	21. Kt. to K. 5th.

White (Mr. Ware).	*Black* (Mr. Mason).
22. P. x B. P.	22. Q. to Q. Kt. sq.
23. Kt. to Q. 4th.	23. Q. x K. P., check.
24. K. to Kt. sq.	24. Q. to K. Kt. 6th.
25. B. to K. 3d.	25. P. to K. 4th.
26. Kt. to B. 3d.	26. B. to Q. B. sq.
27. R. to Q. sq.	27. B. to K. 3d.
28. P. to B. 6th.	28. R. to B. 2d.
29. P. to Q. Kt. 4th.	29. Kt. x Q. B. P.
30. Q. to K. sq.	30. R. x Kt.
31. Q. x Q.	31. R. x Q.
32. B. to K. B. 2d.	32. Kt. x R.
33. B. x R.	33. P. to Q. B. 6th.

And Mr. Ware resigned. (*a*)

NOTE BY W. H. SAYEN.

(*a*) It is but justice to Mr. Ware to state, that in his two games with Mr. Mason, he was laboring under a severe attack of indisposition, and, but for the delay that would have occurred through his absence, he would have kept to his house, instead of being abroad. We have consequently given few notes to either game, as they were too full of glaring oversights on the part of Mr. W.

GAME No. 54.

Played on August 29th, 1876, commencing at 2 P. M.

TIME, 4 HOURS.

Hollandish Opening.

White (Mr. Bird).	*Black* (Mr. Davidson).
1. P. to K. B. 4th. (*a*)	1. P. to Q. 4th.
2. P. to K. 3d.	2. Kt. to Q. B. 3d.
3. Kt. to K. B. 3d.	3. B. to K. Kt. 5th.
4. B. to Q. Kt. 5th.	4. P. to K. 3d.
5. Castles.	5. Kt. to K. B. 3d.
6. P. to K. R. 3d.	6. B. x Kt.
7. Q. x B.	7. P. to Q. R. 3d.
8. B. x Kt.	8. P. x B.
9. P. to Q. Kt. 3d.	9. P. to Q. B. 4th.
10. B. to Q. Kt. 2d.	10. B. to K. 2d.
11. P. to Q. 3d.	11. Castles.
12. Kt. to Q. 2d.	12. R. to Q. Kt. sq.
13. Q. R. to Q. Kt. sq.	13. P. to Q. B. 3d.
14. P. to K. 4th.	14. Kt. to Q. 2d.
15. Q. to K. Kt. 3d. (*b*)	15. B. to K. B. 3d.
16. P. to K. 5th.	16. B. to R. 5th.
17. Q. to K. Kt. 4th.	17. P. to K. Kt. 3d.
18. Kt. to K. B. 3d.	18. B. to K. 2d.
19. P. to K. R. 4th.	19. P. to K. R. 4th.
20. Q. to K. R. 3d.	20. R. to Q. Kt. 5th.
21. P. to K. Kt. 3d.	21. K. to Kt. 2d.

White (Mr. Bird).	*Black* (Mr. Davidson).
22. P. to Q. R. 4th.	22. R. to Q. Kt. 2d.
23. Kt. to K. Kt. 5th.	23. B. x Kt.
24. R. P. x B.	24. Q. to Q. R. 4th.
25. R. to K. B. 2d.	25. Q. to Q. Kt. 5th.
26. Q. R. to K. B. sq.	26. P. to Q. 5th.
27. R. to K. R. 2d.	27. Q. R. to Kt. sq. (*c*)
28. Q. to K. Kt. 2d.	28. Q. R. to Q. B. sq.
29. P. to K. Kt. 4th. (*d*)	29. P. x P.
30. Q. x P.	30. R. to K. R. sq.
31. R. x R.	31. R. x R.
32. Q. to K. Kt. 2d.	32. Kt. to Kt. 3d.
33. B. to B. sq. (*e*)	33. Kt. to Q. 4th.
34. B. to Q. 2d.	34. Q. to Q. Kt. sq.
35. R. to B. 3d.	35. R. to R. 5th.
36. R. to R. 3d. (*f*)	36. Kt. x P. (*g*)
37. B. x Kt.	37. R. x B.
38. R. to R. 7th, check.	38. K. x R. (*h*)
39. Q. to R. 2d, check.	39. K. to Kt. sq.
40. Q. x R.	40. Q. to Kt. 5th.
41. Q. to B. 2d.	41. Q. to R. 6th. (*i*)

And the game was abandoned as drawn.

NOTES BY W. H. SAYEN.

(*a*) In a previous game we have given our opinion, and that of others, on this style of opening.

(*b*) We could here have wished to see the effects of P. to K. B. 5th, followed by P. to K. Kt. 4th, and a general attack with the King's Pawns. The play adopted was safer, and therefore yielded but negative results.

(*c*) In order to play K. R. to K. sq., should White play P. to K. Kt. 4th.

(*d*) A very weak move, which gives Black the advantage.

(*e*) Had White taken the offered Pawn he would have lost the game, *i. e.* :—

33. Q. x Q. B. P.	33. Kt. to Q. 4th.
34. B. to Q. B. sq.	34. Q. to B. 6th,

and White cannot save the game.

(*f*) This move is played with great skill, but should have lost.

(*g*) We here prefer Q. to K. R. sq., followed by 37. Q. to R. 4th.

(*h*) He must take the Rook or be mated.

(*i*) Better Q. to B. 6th.

GAME No. 55.

Played on August 30th, 1876, commencing at 9 A. M.

TIME, 6 HOURS.

Hollandish Opening.

White (Mr. Bird).	*Black* (Mr. Elson).
1. P. to K. B. 4th.	1. P. to Q. 4th.
2. P. to K. 3d.	2. P. to K. B. 4th.
3. B. to K. 2d.	3. Kt. to K. B. 3d.
4. Kt. to K. B. 3d.	4. P. to K. 3d.
5. P. to Q. Kt. 3d.	5. B. to K. 2d.
6. B. to Q. Kt. 2d.	6. Castles.
7. Kt. to Q. R. 3d.	7. Kt. to K. 5th.
8. Castles.	8. B. to K. B. 3d.
9. P. to Q. B. 3d.	9. Q. to K. 2d.
10. Kt. to Q. B. 2d.	10. P. to Q. B. 4th.
11. Q. to K. sq.	11. Kt. to Q. B. 3d.
12. P. to Q. 3d.	12. Kt. to Q. 3d.
13. P. to Q. 4th.	13. Kt. to K. 5th. (*a*)
14. B. to Q. R. 3d.	14. P. to Q. Kt. 3d.
15. B. to Q. 3d.	15. Q. to Q. sq.
16. Q. R. to Q. sq.	16. B. to Q. Kt. 2d.
17. Kt. to K. 5th.	17. B. to K. 2d.
18. B. x Kt.	18. B. P. x B.
19. Kt. x Kt.	19. B. x Kt.

White (Mr. Bird).	*Black* (Mr. Elson).
20. P. to Q. B. 4th.	20. Q. to Q. B. 2d.
21. Q. to K. 2d.	21. R. to K. B. 3d.
22. Q. P. x P.	22. Kt. P. x P.
23. B. to Q. Kt. 2d.	23. R. to K. R. 3d.
24. P. to K. Kt. 4th.	24. R. to K. Kt. 3d. (*b*)
25. P. x Q. P.	25. P. x P.
26. P. to K. B. 5th.	26. R. to K. R. 3d.
27. R. to K. B. 2d.	27. Q. R. to K. B. sq.
28. R. to K. Kt. 2d.	28. B. to K. Kt. 4th.
29. B. to B. 3d.	29. R. to R. 6th.
30. B. to K. sq.	30. R. to K. sq.
31. B. to Kt. 3d.	31. Q. to Q. Kt. 3d.
32. P. to Q. Kt. 4th. (*c*)	32. P. x P.
33. Kt. to Q. 4th.	33. P. to Q. R. 4th.
34. R. to K. B. 2d.	34. R. to Q. B. sq.
35. K. to Kt. 2d.	35. R. to R. 3d.
36. K. R. to K. B. sq.	36. B. to Q. R. 5th.
37. R. to Q. B. sq.	37. R. to Q. B. 6th.
38. R. x R.	38. P. x R.
39. P. to K. R. 4th. (*d*)	39. B. x P.
40. B. to K. B. 4th.	40. B. to K. B. 3d. (*e*)
41. B. x R.	41. B. x Kt.
42. P. x B.	42. B. to Q. Kt. 4th.
43. P. to B. 6th. (*f*)	43. P. x B.
44. R. to Q. Kt. sq. (*g*)	44. B. x Q.
45. R. x Q.	45. P. to B. 7th.

And Mr. Bird resigns.

NOTES BY JACOB ELSON.

(*a*) Seemingly good, but in reality of doubtful merit. White should, in reply to this move, have taken P. with P., and on

Black retaking with Kt., played the B. to R. 3d; when the following variation would have occurred:—

	13. Kt. to K. 5th.
14. P. x P.	14. Kt. x P.
15. B. to Q. R. 3d.	15. Kt. to Q., best.
16. P. to Q. Kt. 4th.	16. Kt. to K. 5th.
17. P. to Kt. 5th.	17. Kt. to Q. 3d.

And, although Black loses nothing, yet his position is uncomfortable.

(*b*) It seems exceedingly difficult to hit upon the right move for Black at this juncture. The move in the text was made to induce P. to K. B. 5th on the part of White, after the exchange of Pawns, when (as in reality happened) R. to R. 3d, followed up by B. to Kt. 4th, would give Black a strong game.

(*c*) This move was almost compulsory to prevent the threatened advance of Black's centre pawns.

(*d*) The initiatory step of a fine combination, which, but for the great caution on the part of Black, would most likely have won the game.

(*e*) The correct move, and one which will repay close examination. Play as White may, Black will now retain the advantage.

(*f*) The end game is one of singular beauty. If Black now takes the Queen, White mates in some five or six moves, by P. to B. 7th, check, followed up by B. x P., check, *a. s. f.*

(*g*) Fatal. But no play can save White's game. If White, instead of 43. P. to B. 6th, had played R. to Q. Kt. sq. at once, then follows:—

	43. B. x Q.
44. R. x Q.	44. P. x B.
45. R. to Q. Kt. sq.	45. P. to B. 7th.
46. R. to Q. B. sq.	46. B. to Q. 8th.

And Black must win.

GAME No. 56.

Played on August 30th, 1876, commencing at 2 P.M.

TIME, 4 HOURS.

Ruy Lopez's Knight's Game.

White (Mr. Elson).	*Black* (Mr. Bird).
1. P. to K. 4th.	1. P. to K. 4th.
2. Kt. to K. B. 3d.	2. Kt. to Q. B. 3d.
3. B. to Q. Kt. 5th.	3. Kt. to Q. 5th. (*a*)
4. B. to B. 4th. (*b*)	4. Q. to K. B. 3d.
5. P. to Q. B. 3d.	5. Kt. x Kt., check.
6. Q. x Kt.	6. B. to Q. B. 4th.
7. P. to Q. 3d.	7. P. to Q. 3d.
8. B. to K. 3d.	8. Q. x Q.
9. P. x Q.	9. B. x B.
10. P. x B.	10. B. to K. 3d.
11. Kt. to Q. 2d.	11. Kt. to K. B. 3d.
12. P. to Q. 4th.	12. B. x B.
13. Kt. x B.	13. Kt. to Q. 2d.
14. K. to K. 2d.	14. Castles Q. R.
15. P. to Q. R. 4th.	15. K. R. to K. sq.
16. K. to Q. 3d.	16. P. to K. Kt. 3d.
17. P. to Q. Kt. 4th.	17. Kt. to K. B. 3d.
18. K. R. to K. B. sq.	18. R. to K. 2d.
19. Q. to [illegible] K. sq.	19. Q. R. to K. sq.
20. P. to Q. R. 5th.	20. Kt. to Q. 2d.
21. Kt. to Q. 2d.	21. K. P. x Q. P.

White (Mr. Elson).	*Black* (Mr. Bird).
22. K. P. x Q. P.	22. P. to K. B. 4th.
23. R. to B. 2d.	23. Kt. to K. B. 3d.
24. R. fr. B. 2d to K. 2d.	24. Kt. to R. 4th.
25. K. to Q. B. 2d. (*c*)	25. Kt. to K. B. 5th.
26. R. to K. B. 2d.	26. P. to Q. Kt. 4th.
27. P. to K. R. 4th.	27. P. to Q. R. 3d.
28. R. to K. R. 2d.	28. K. to Kt. 2d.
29. R. to K. Kt. sq.	29. P. to Q. B. 3d.
30. R. to Kt. 5th.	30. P. to K. R. 3d.
31. R. to Kt. sq.	31. K. to Q. B. 2d.
32. P. x P.	32. P. x P.
33. P. to R. 5th.	33. R. to K. 7th.
34. R. x R.	34. R. x R.
35. R. to Kt. 7th, check.	35. K. to Kt. sq.
36. R. to K. R. 7th.	36. R. to K. 3d.
37. R. to K. B. 7th.	37. Kt. x R. P.
38. R. x B. P.	38. Kt. to K. B. 3d.

Drawn game.

NOTES BY JACOB ELSON.

(*a*) This move is a specialty with Mr. Bird, who has successfully adopted it against the great masters of Europe, including Mr. Anderssen, whom he defeated in a game at this opening at the Vienna Congress. The books generally pronounce the move a bad one, but Mr. Bird has shown wonderful resource and originality in his management of it.

(*b*) Made wise by a previous experience, White preferred retreating the B. to the capture of the Kt.

(*c*) Great caution on the part of White was necessary at this juncture.

GAME No. 57.

Played on August 31st, 1876, commencing at 9 A.M.

TIME, 4 HOURS.

Irregular Opening.

White (Mr. Davidson).	*Black* (Mr. Ware).
1. P. to Q. B. 4th. (*a*)	1. P. to Q. 4th.
2. P. to K. 3d.	2. P. to Q. B. 3d.
3. P. to Q. 4th.	3. P. to K. B. 4th. (*b*)
4. Q. Kt. to B. 3d. (*c*)	4. K. Kt. to B. 3d.
5. K. Kt. to B. 3d.	5. P. to K. 3d.
6. P. to Q. R. 3d.	6. B. to K. 2d. (*d*)
7. B. to Q. 3d.	7. P. to Q. R. 3d.
8. Castles.	8. Castles.
9. Kt. to K. 5th.	9. Q. Kt. to Q. 2d.
10. Kt. to K. 2d. (*e*)	10. Kt. x Kt.
11. P. x Kt.	11. Kt. to Kt. 5th.
12. P. to K. B. 4th.	12. B. to B. 4th.
13. Kt. to Q. 4th.	13. B. to Q. 2d. (*f*)
14. P. to K. R. 3d.	14. Kt. to R. 3d.
15. P. to Q. Kt. 4th.	15. B. x Kt.
16. P. x B.	16. Kt. to K. B. 2d.
17. P. to B. 5th.	17. Q. to R. 5th.
18. B. to Q. 2d.	18. K. to R. sq. (*g*)
19. K. to R. 2d.	19. Kt. to R. 3d.
20. B. to K. sq.	20. Q. to K. 2d.

White (Mr. Davidson).	*Black* (Mr. Ware).
21. R. to R. 2d.	21. B. to K. sq.
22. P. to K. Kt. 3d. (*h*)	22. Kt. to Kt. sq.
23. R. to K. Kt. 2d.	23. P. to K. Kt. 3d.
24. P. to Kt. 4th.	24. Kt. to R. 3d.
25. P. x P.	25. Kt. P. x P.
26. R. to Kt. 5th.	26. B. to Kt. 3d.
27. K. R. to Kt. sq.	27. Q. to K. B. 2d.
28. B. to R. 4th.	28. Q. to Kt. 2d.
29. B. to K. 2d. (*i*)	29. R. to B. 2d.
30. B. to R. 5th.	30. Q. R. to K. Kt. sq.
31. B. x B. (*j*)	31. P. x B.
32. R. x P. (*k*)	32. Q. x R.
33. R. x Q.	33. R. x R.
34. B. to B. 6th, check.	34. K. to R. 2d.
35. Q. to K. 2d.	35. R. to K. B. sq.
36. P. to Q. R. 4th. (*l*)	36. Q. R. to K. Kt. sq.
37. B. to Kt. 5th.	37. Kt. to B. 2d.
38. P. to K. R. 4th.	38. Kt. to R. 3d.
39. P. to Q. Kt. 5th. (*m*)	39. Kt. to Kt. 5th, check.
40. K. to Kt. 3d.	40. R. P. x P.
41. P. x P.	41. R. to Q. R. sq.
42. Q. to Kt. 2d.	42. R. to K. Kt. 2d.
43. K. to B. 3d.	43. R. to Q. 2d.
44. P. to R. 5th.	44. R. to B. 2d.
45. B. to B. 6th.?	45. K. to R. 3d.
46. B. to Kt. 5th, check.	46. K. x R. P.
47. P. x P.	47. P. x P.
48. Q. to Kt. 6th.	48. R. fr. B. 2d to Kt. 2d.
49. Q. x P.	49. R. to R. 7th.

And White resigned.

NOTES BY W. H. SAYEN.

(*a*) We much prefer this move, in close openings, to P. to K. B. 4th.

(*b*) This move cannot be regarded as anything but weak, leaving, as it does, the K. P. so unprotected in the end game.

(*c*) Here we prefer exchanging the less valuable Q. B. P. for the Q. P., freeing the action of the K. B., and giving a slightly preferable position, *i. e.* :—

4. P. x Q. P.	4. P. x P.
5. K. Kt. to B. 3d.	5. P. to K. 3d.
6. P. to Q. R. 3d.	6. K. Kt. to B. 3d.
7. B. to Q. 3d.	7. B. to Q. 3d.
8. Castles.	8. Castles.
9. Kt. to Q. 2d.	9. Kt. to Q. B. 3d.
10. P. to Q. Kt. 4th.	10. P. to Q. R. 3d.

11. Kt. to Q. Kt. 3d, and we prefer White's game.

(*d*) Mr. Steinitz always prefers B. to Q. 3d in close positions of this kind.

(*e*) Better Kt. x Kt., followed by P. to B. 5th and Kt. to Q. R. 4th.

(*f*) Black could here have played B. x Kt. with advantage, *i. e.* :—

	13. B. x Kt.
14. P. x B.	14. P. to Q. Kt. 4th.
15. P. to B. 5th.	15. P. to Q. R. 4th, etc.

He might also have played 13. Q. to Q. Kt. 3d.

(*g*) 18. P. to K. Kt. 4th will bear analysis. The King could have been housed safely at R. 2d, and both Rooks deployed on the K. Kt. file.

(*h*) From this point Mr. Davidson gains a fine position.

(*i*) Q. to R. 5th would have been answered by R. to K. Kt. sq.

(*j*) A blunder. R. from Kt. 5th to Kt. 3d was the correct play, and we do not see how Black could avert loss, *i. e.* :—

31. R. to K. Kt. 3d.	31. B. x B.
32. Q. x B.	32. Q. to B. sq.
33. B. to B. 6th, check, and wins.	
Or if	31. Q. to B. sq.
32. B. to B. 6th, check, and wins.	

(*k*) Though winning a Pawn, it was extremely injudicious to exchange the Queen for two Rooks in an end game.

(*l*) The attempt to break through the Queen's side, exposing himself as he did to the attack of the Rooks, cost White the game. B. to K. Kt. 5th, followed by Q. to R. 5th, finally exchanging the B. for the Kt., and endeavoring to gain the opposition by exchanging the Q. and the K. R. P. for the two Rooks at K. R. 6th, might have won.

(*m*) Virtually losing the game. He had but a draw, and in match play, any attempt to force a position which, according to all known principles and analyses, is drawn, generally loses.

GAME No. 58.

Played on August 31st, 1876, commencing at 2 P. M.

TIME, 2 HOURS.

Irregular Opening.

White (Mr. Ware).	*Black* (Mr. Davidson).
1. P. to Q. 4th.	1. P. to K. 3d.
2. P. to K. B. 4th.	2. P. to Q. 4th.
3. Kt. to K. B. 3d.	3. P. to Q. B. 4th.
4. P. to Q. B. 3d. (*a*)	4. Kt. to Q. B. 3d.
5. P. to K. 3d.	5. P. to Q. R. 3d.
6. B. to K. 2d.	6. Kt. to B. 3d.
7. P. to Q. R. 3d.	7. Kt. to K. 5th.
8. Q. Kt. to Q. 2d.	8. P. to K. B. 4th.
9. Castles.	9. B. to K. 2d.
10. Kt. x Kt.	10. B. P. x Kt.
11. Kt. to K. 5th.	11. Castles.
12. B. to Q. 2d.	12. B. to Q. 2d.
13. P. to Q. Kt. 4th.	13. P. x Q. P.
14. Kt. x Kt.	14. Kt. P. x Kt.
15. B. P. x P.	15. Q. to B. 2d.
16. Q. to B. 2d.	16. P. to K. Kt. 4th. (*b*)
17. P. to K. Kt. 3d.	17. K. to R. sq.
18. K. to R. sq.	18. P. x B. P.
19. Kt. P. x P.	19. R. to B. 3d.
20. R. to K. Kt. sq.	20. R. to R. 3d.
21. R. to Kt. 2d.	21. B. to B. 3d.

White (Mr. Ware).	*Black* (Mr. Davidson).
22. Q. R. to K. Kt. sq.	22. Q. to Q. sq.
23. B. to K. sq. (*c*)	23. Q. to K. 2d. (*d*)
24. B. x Q. R. P.	24. R. to K. Kt. 3d. (*e*)
25. R. x R.	25. P. x R.
26. B. to K. B. sq. (*f*)	26. R. x R. P.
27. Q. to K. B. 2d. (*g*)	27. K. to Kt. 2d.
28. B. to K. 2d.	28. R. to Q. R. sq.
29. B. to K. R. 5th.	29. B. to K. sq.
30. P. to B. 5th.	30. P. to Kt. 4th.
31. B. to K. Kt. 4th.	31. B. to B. 2d.
32. R. to Kt. 2d.	32. R. to K. R. sq.
33. Q. to Kt. 3d. (*h*)	33. P. to K. 4th. (*i*)
34. B. to Q. B. 3d.	34. P. x P.
35. P. x P.	35. Q. to R. 2d.
36. Q. to K. 3d.	36. Q. to Q. Kt. sq.
37. B. to K. 2d.	37. K. to B. sq.
38. Q. to K. Kt. 3d.	38. Q. x Q.
39. R. x Q.	39. B. to R. 4th.
40. B. to Q. R. 6th.	40. R. to R. 2d.
41. K. to Kt. sq.	41. R. to Q. R. 2d.
42. P. to Kt. 5th.	42. B. to K. 7th.
43. B. to Kt. 4th, check.	43. K. to K. sq.
44. B. to B. 5th.	44. R. to K. Kt. 2d. (*j*)
45. R. to Q. Kt. 3d.	45. P. x P.
46. B. x P., check.	46. B. x B.
47. R. x B.	47. R. to Q. 2d.
48. K. to B. 2d.	48. B. to K. 2d.
49. K. to K. 3d.	49. K. to B. 2d.
50. R. to Kt. 6th.	50. B. to Q. sq.
51. R. to R. 6th.	51. B. to B. 2d.
52. P. to K. R. 3d.	52. B. to B. 5th, check.
53. K. to K. 2d.	53. R. to Q. Kt. 2d.

White (Mr. Ware).	*Black* (Mr. Davidson).
54. R. to R. 7th. (*k*)	54. R. x R.
55. B. x R.	55. K. to B. 3d
56. B. to B. 5th.	56. K. x P.
57. B. to Kt. 4th.	57. B. to Kt. 6th.
58. B. to Q. 2d.	58. K. to Kt. 3d. (*l*)
59. K. to B. sq.	59. K. to R. 4th.
60. K. to Kt. 2d.	60. B. to B. 5th.
61. B. to B. 3d.	61. K. to Kt. 3d. (*m*)
62. K. to B. 2d.	62. K. to B. 4th.
63. K. to K. 2d.	63. K. to K. 3d.
64. K. to Q. sq.	64. K. to Q. 3d.
65. K. to B. 2d.	65. K. to B. 3d.
66. K. to Kt. 3d.	66. K. to Kt. 4th.
67. B. to K. sq.	67. B. to K. 6th.
68. B. to B. 6th.	68. B. to B. 7th.
69. B. to Kt. 2d.	69. P. to K. 6th.

And White resigned.

NOTES BY W. H. SAYEN.

(*a*) P. to Q. Kt. 3d, followed by B. to Kt. 2d, frequently gives a good game in close openings. It also prevents P. to Q. B. 5th.

(*b*) Taking the initiative, which leads to some fine positions.

(*c*) Of course it would have been imprudent to exchange the Rooks for the Queen. We, however, prefer B. to Q. B. sq. to the move in the text, protecting the Q. R. P. in the event of capturing, as afterwards happened, the Q. R. P. of Black.

(*d*) A bad move; yet it was difficult to see what to do. B. to Q. B. might have been played, followed by B. to Q. Kt. 2d.

(*e*) Apparently the only move.

(*f*) Losing the golden opportunity. He should have played 26. R. x Kt. P., *i. e.* :—

26. R. x Kt. P.	26. R. x B. (1)
27. Q. to K. 2d, and wins.	
Or (1)	26. K. to R. 2d. (2)
27. Q. to K. Kt. 2d.	27. Q. to K. B. 2d.
28. R. to K. Kt. 4th, and wins.	

(2)

	26. B. to K. sq.
27. R. to K. Kt. 3d.	27. R. x B.
28. Q. to K. 2d.	28. R. to R. sq., best.
29. Q. to K. Kt. 4th.	29. Q. to K. Kt. 2d.
30. R. to R. 3d, check.	30. K. to Kt. sq.
31. Q. x K. P., check, and wins.	

(*g*) Again R. x K. Kt. P. would have been safe play, but involved many intricate combinations.

(*h*) Much better to have exchanged the P. and B., and then assaulted the K. Kt. P.

(*i*) Correctly played. Black now secures a decided advantage.

(*j*) If R. to R. sq., White answers R. to Q. R. 3d.

(*k*) This loses at once the B. P. Better R. to R. 8th or P. to B. 6th, followed by B. to K. 7th or else B. to Kt. 6th, followed by B. to Q. 8th, *i. e.* :—

54. B. to Kt. 6th.	54. If K. to B. 3d.
55. B. to Q. 8th, check, and at least draws.	

(*l*) Better P. to Kt. 5th at once.

(*m*) B. to K. 6th would have won more easily.

GAME No. 59.

Played on August 31st, 1876, commencing at 9 A. M.

TIME, 5 HOURS.

French Defence.

White (Mr. Judd).	*Black* (Mr. Mason).
1. P. to K. 4th.	1. P. to K. 3d.
2. K. to K. B. 3d.	2. P. to Q. 4th.
3. P. x P.	3. P. x P.
4. P. to Q. 4th. (*a*)	4. Kt. to K. B. 3d.
5. B. to Q. 3d.	5. B. to Q. 3d.
6. Castles.	6. Castles.
7. P. to K. R. 3d. (*b*)	7. B. to K. 3d.
8. Q. Kt. to B. 3d. (*c*)	8. P. to B. 3d.
9. B. to K. 3d.	9. Q. to B. 2d.
10. Kt. to K. R. 4th.	10. Q. Kt. to Q. 2d.
11. P. to K. B. 4th. (*d*)	11. Kt. to Kt. 3d.
12. P. to Q. Kt. 3d.	12. Q. R. to K. sq.
13. B. to Q. 2d.	13. B. to B. sq.
14. Q. to B. 3d.	14. Q to K. 2d.
15. Kt. to B. 5th.	15. B. x Kt.
16. B. x B.	16. Kt. to K. 5th. (*e*)
17. B. x Kt.	17. P. x B.
18. Q. to Kt. 3d.	18. P. to K. B. 4th.
19. B. to K. 3d.	19. R. to B. 3d.
20. Q. to B. 2d.	20. R. to Kt. 3d.
21. Q. R. to Q. sq.	21. B. to Kt. 5th.

White (Mr. Judd).	*Black* (Mr. Mason).
22. Kt. to K. 2d.	22. Kt. to Q. 4th.
23. P. to Q. B. 4th. (*f*)	23. Kt. x B.
24. Q. x Kt.	24. B. to R. 4th.
25. P. to Q. R. 4th.	25. B. to Kt. 3d.
26. R. to Q. 2d.	26. B. to R. 4th.
27. R. to B. 2d.	27. R. to Q. sq.
28. R to Q. sq.	28. K. R. to Q. 3d.
29. K. to R. sq.	29. R. fr. Q. 3d to Q. 2d.
30. R. fr. B. 2d to B. sq. (*g*)	30. B. to B. 2d.
31. P. to Kt. 3d.	31. B. to R. 4th. (*h*)
32. K. to Kt. 2d.	32. Q. to B. 3d.
33. P. to K. R. 4th.	33. B. to Kt. 5th.
34. R. to Q. Kt. sq.	34. B. to B. 4th. (*i*)
35. P. to Q. Kt. 4th.	35. B. x P.
36. Kt. x B.	36. R. x Kt.
37. R. x R.	37. Q. x R.
38. Q. x Q.	38. R. x Q. (*j*)
39. R. to Q. B. sq.	39. K. to B. 2d.
40. K. to B. 2d.	40. R. to Q. 6th.
41. R. to B. 2d.	41. K. to Kt. 3d.
42. K. to Kt. 2d.	42. K. to R. 4th.
43. K. to R. 3d.	43. P. to K. R. 3d.
44. P. to B. 5th.	44. R. to R. 3d.
45. R. to Q. 2d.	45. R. to Q. 6th. (*k*)
46. R. to Q. Kt. 2d.	46. P. to K. Kt. 4th.
47. B. P. x. P.	47. P. x P.
48. R. to K. B. 2d.	48. P. to B. 5th.

And Black wins. (*l*)

NOTES BY W. H. SAYEN.

(*a*) This brings about the original French Defence. We prefer this to the modern Q. Kt. to B. 3d on White's 3d move.

(*b*) The *Handbuch* here prefers Q. Kt. to B. 3d, followed by Q. B. to K. Kt. 5th.

(*c*) We prefer 8. Q. Kt. to Q. 2d, 9. Kt. to Kt. 3d.

(*d*) We cannot commend this move. Besides leaving a free and open file for the Black K. B., the pawn also is weakened, as the K. Kt. P. cannot be thrown forward to its support, on account of the position of the Black Queen and K. B.

(*e*) The manner in which Mr. Mason manœuvres to secure a passed Pawn, is worthy of study.

(*f*) An ill-considered move, which subsequently loses the Q. P. Perhaps R. to Q. B., followed by P. to Q. B. 3d, would have given better results.

(*g*) To prevent B. to Kt. 3d and its fatal effects.

(*h*) In some of these moves, both sides were pressed for time. White, however, should have played R. to Q. B. 2d on his 32d move instead of K. to Kt. 2d.

(*i*) He had no escape from the attack of this Bishop.

(*j*) These exchanges are certainly not favorable to White.

(*k*) Correctly played. White would have given him much trouble had the Rook been permitted to go to Q. 7th.

(*l*) The game was continued a few more moves, but Mr. Mason won easily by means of his superiority of Pawns.

GAME No. 60.

This game was the first of two games played to decide the tie between these players. Each won one, and the second was not handed in, in time, by Mr. Elson, for publication.

French Defence.

White (Mr. Davidson).	*Black* (Mr. Elson).
1. P. to K. 4th.	1. P. to K. 3d.
2. Kt. to Q. B. 3d.	2. P. to Q. 4th.
3. P. x P.	3. P. x P.
4. P. to Q. 4th.	4 Kt. to K. B. 3d.
5. B. to K. Kt. 5th.	5. B. to Q. Kt. 5th.
6. Q. to K. 2d, check.	6. B. to K. 3d.
7. Q. to Kt. 5th, check.	7. Kt. to Q. B. 3d.
8. Kt. to K. B. 3d. (*a*)	8. Q. to Q. 2d.
9. B. x Kt.	9. P. x B.
10. Q. x Kt. P.	10. R. to Q. Kt. sq.
11. Q. to R. 3d.	11. R. to Q. Kt. 3d.
12. Q. to R. 4th. (*b*)	12. Castles. (*c*)
13. P. to Q. R. 3d.	13. B. x Kt., check. (*d*)
14. P. x B.	14. K. R. to Q. Kt.
15. B. to Q. 3d.	15. B. to K. Kt. 5th.
16. Castles. (*e*)	16. B. x Kt.
17. P. x B.	17. Q. to K. R. 6th.
18. K. R. to K. sq. (*f*)	18. K. to R. sq.
19. K. to R. sq.	19. Q. x B. P., check. (*g*)
20. K. to Kt. sq.	20. R. to Kt., check.

White (Mr. DAVIDSON).	*Black* (Mr. ELSON).
21. K. to B. sq.	21. R. to Kt. 7th.
22. R. to K. 2d.	22. R. x R. P.
Resigns.	

NOTES BY JACOB ELSON.

(*a*) This move secures the winning of Q. Kt. P., as any attempt on the part of Black to save it would result disastrously. Had White instead of this move played 8. Q. x Kt. P. at once, Black would have replied 8. Kt. x Q. P., as White does not take B. with Q. on account of Kt. x B. P., check. The winning of Q. Kt. P. with Q., however, in the early stages of the game is seldom a boon, and the present instance forms no exception to the general rule.

(*b*) This move is objectionable, as it confines the Q. to the Q. side, and makes it very problematical if she can be brought over to the King's side, should the tide of battle turn that way. Q. to Q. 3d, however, would have been replied to by B. to K. B. 4th and Q. to Q. 2d by B. to Q. R. 4th.

(*c*) Threatening Kt. x Q. P.

(*d*) B. to Q. R. 4th came into consideration here, if then White played P. to Q. Kt. 4th, Black replies Kt. x Kt. P., with a very fine attack.

(*e*) Kt. to Q. 2d seems to be better. This move seriously compromises White's game.

(*f*) Fatal. B. to K. 2d, or P. to K. B. 4th, would either of them have given White a better chance to escape.

(*g*) Black, seeing one road to victory, overlooks the shorter one of R. to K. Kt. sq.

www.ingramcontent.com/pod-product-compliance
Lightning Source LLC
Chambersburg PA
CBHW031059280326
41928CB00049B/1111
9783337221478